W9-BZQ-459

FORTUNE-TELLING BY PLAYING CARDS

Using playing cards to interpret the definite psychic relationship which exists between man and his environment, this book shows how secrets of the future, symbolized in the cards, may be disclosed for self-improvement and self-knowledge in the present.

FORTUNE-TELLING BY PLAYING CARDS

A New Guide to the Ancient Art of Cartomancy

by

NERYS DEE

Sterling Publishing Co., Inc.   New York

9 10 8

Published in 1990 by Sterling Publishing Company, Inc.
387 Park Avenue South, New York, N.Y. 10016
Originally published in Great Britain by The Aquarian Press
© 1982 by Nerys Dee
Distributed in Canada by Sterling Publishing
% Canadian Manda Group, P. O. Box 920, Station U
Toronto, Ontario, Canada M8Z 5P9
Manufactured in the United States of America

ISBN 0-85030-266-8

CONTENTS

The author and publisher are greatly indebted to Waddingtons Playing Card Company for permission to reproduce their playing cards which are illustrated in this book.

INTRODUCTION

Cartomancy, or fortune-telling with the cards, is as old as the hills. Ancient civilizations throughout the world once consulted them in search of answers to their problems and right up to the Middle Ages they were accepted as oracles of wisdom by both State and Church.

By the seventeenth century they were even more popular but in a very different way. Seeing them as a quick and easy way to win money, not to mention lose it, the cards became the gamblers' delight, with a result that their true purpose of divination was completely overshadowed. It was this new-found gambling role that led the Victorians to rank them with drunkenness, bawdiness and sex, banning and denouncing them as evil. This gave them the long-lingering, unworthy image that has persisted, to some extent, to this very day. Even so, their secret tradition was not lost for it was kept alive during these years by lone mystics and by gypsies, well known for their fortune-telling with the cards.

Unfortunately, just when the shackles of an ignorant society were about to be thrown off, at the beginning of this century, along came an even more formidable opponent in the form of science. This body applied its type of logic and announced that there was absolutely no connection whatsoever between a few playing cards and events from the past, let alone associations with the future.

Fortunately, individual experiences and computerized results from random selections of cards have since proved, without a shadow of doubt, that science does not, by a long way, hold all the aces. This proof is further supported by the work of C. G. Jung who showed that a definite psychic relationship exists between man and his environment. It is this unseen link that is responsible for all those intriguing coincidences which frequently occur in our lives. Jung named these happenings 'synchronistic events' and it was this discovery that led him to investigate the mystery and wisdom underlying not only the cards but all forms of divination, from the *I Ching* to tea-leaves.

Today, the cards have once again taken their rightful place in society. With a little practice everyone can receive and understand their symbolic messages which reveal hidden personal talents, future emotional happiness, financial situations and pitfalls which are meant to be avoided. There is, in fact, no need to fear what might be revealed by the cards for they are blessings in disguise; remember that to be forewarned is to be forearmed. Fate and fortune shown in this way help you to 'play your cards right' in relation to the game of life itself and give you a much better chance of winning each round hands down.

1

THE ORIGIN OF THE CARDS

The goddess Fortune, it is said, frustrates single-handed the plans of a thousand learned men. To outwit her has been a human pursuit since the dawn of time and, although oracles have come and oracles have gone, divination through the cards has survived, virtually unaltered, to this very day.

The origin of the 52 playing cards is now lost in the mists of time, but it seems probable that it stems from the same mysterious source as that of the tarot and chess. It is often suggested that the playing cards are descendants of the tarot pack itself, but their amazing numerical significance in relation to the solar system, the universe and time seems to give them an importance entirely in their own right.

There is, of course, a close relationship between the 52 playing cards and the 56 cards that go to make up the Minor Arcana of the tarot pack. Both sets have four suits. Each suit contains ten numbered cards plus court cards; there are twelve in the 52-card pack and sixteen in the 56 tarot pack. It is the four extra court cards in the Minor Arcana that completely destroy the obvious yet unique significance associated with the number 52.

In the fourteenth century the 52-card pack was given four additional court cards and annexed to the 22 cards known as the Major Arcana. This made up the 78-card tarot pack we know today. Before this time, the tarot, representing the Qabalistic Tree of Life, consisted of the 22 major trumps only.

Ancient civilizations once had their own versions of the cards. The Chinese engraved copper and silver plates with designs and numbers based on the four suits, which they then reproduced on paper, making them into what is believed to be the very first pack of cards. Later, by introducing the Tao principle of Yin and Yang, black and white, they devised the game we now know as chess. This requires considerable mental skill, patience and foresight for, like the cards, it symbolizes the game of life itself with its surprise encounters and counter-moves.

It is said that the Indians knew of the cards at this time too, with theirs depicting Hindu deities holding swords, sceptres, cups and rings. If this is so, then Ireland may also be considered as the originator of the four suits because this is the homeland of the four prehistoric grails – the sword, the sceptre, the cup and the ring.

Japan, Korea, North and South America and the Pacific Islands have also been credited with introducing the cards to mankind, but it is from Egypt that we find most evidence concerning them in their earliest form. Even so, this still does not give sufficient proof to show that Egypt was the land of their origin. And from here, our trail leads us back to Atlantis, but that is another story.

Court de Gebelin in the eighteenth century wrote: 'If it were known that there existed today a work of the ancient Egyptians which escaped the flames that devoured their superb libraries and which contains their purest doctrines on the most profound and interesting subjects, everyone would doubtless be anxious to acquire the secrets from so valuable a work.'

He was, in fact, referring to *The Book of Thoth,* from which our present day cards are derived. This book is said to contain all the answers to mankind's problems and is made up of a series of plates engraved with hieroglyphics, based on an alphabet depicting gods as letters, letters as ideas, ideas as numbers and numbers as perfect signs. The priests are thought to have assembled this work after consultation with their god of magic, Thoth. They decided to hide within its ancient pages timeless secrets which would always be accessible to future generations, provided they had the desire to seek out such knowledge and wisdom. These same priests also decided that the best way to hide these eternal secrets, yet at the same time keep them within reach of everyone, was to appeal to the vice in man as well as to his nobler qualities. This, then, is why the cards today still carry the profoundest of messages on the one hand, yet are found spread over the seamiest gambling tables of the world on the other.

From Egypt comes the story of yet another book supposedly written by Hermes whose life and times pre-date the pyramids by many centuries. This is said to have contained gold leaves, each of which was impressed with numbers and letters similar to those in *The Book of Thoth.* Together these constituted the Arcanum or secret wisdom of the world. It is

to Simeon ben Jochai, a Jewish initiate, that we owe all know-
ledge of this book, now known as *The Hermetic Book of
Destiny*. It was, incidentally, at the command of Pope Clement
XIV that Simeon ben Jochai translated it into Latin.

It is said that Moses, who was well versed in Egyptian lore
and magic, took *The Book of Thoth* with him when he and the
children of Israel left Egypt in search of the Promised land.
This he guarded carefully, but after many years it appeared in
the Middle East as a text known as the 'taro'. There is seen in
this a close connection between the 'taro' and the 'tora', which
is, of course, the Hebrew law code in the Old Testament.
There is also a close connection between the 'taro' and 'rota',
(the wheel of time and fortune). By rearranging the letters
alone – tora, taro and rota – we see a glimpse of the magic of
the cards and, although the absolute interpretations of both the
books of Thoth and Hermes are now lost, we still have the
keys to unlock many of their mysteries in our present day 52
playing cards and the 22 cards of the Major Arcana.

2

THE HISTORY OF THE CARDS

The cards made their first appearance in Europe around the eleventh century. Exactly how they arrived and who brought them has given rise to almost as many legends as their origin itself, but at least we are certain of one thing and that is that they were not invented by a member of the French court to amuse a bored king.

From A.D. 1200 onwards, Europe has played host to an ever increasing number of travellers from all over the world. Routes between Mediterranean countries, Asia Minor and the Far East were opened up, enabling merchants to bring to the West their exotic goods from lands as far away as India and China. Trade links were formed with Islamic countries too, so it is virtually impossible to discover which of these newcomers actually brought the famous cards with them.

Some sources say it was the Saracens or 'gypsies' – a corruption of 'Egyptians' – whilst other authorities insist it was the Chinese. Although this may have been the case, it is more likely that the Knights Templars were responsible, having learned about them from the Saracens during their crusades to the Holy Land. On their return to England they certainly made no secret of their knowledge of the cards for, in 1230, the Synod of Worcester forbad the Knights to play a card game they called 'King and Queen'.

Until the fifteenth century the cards were alternately banned and approved by heads of State and the Church, both in England and throughout Europe. In France, Italy and England they were as popular within monastic walls as they were with royalty at court and only later did members of the public become familiar with them. So far as England is concerned, if the Knights Templars did not bring the cards, then they reached these shores from France, where they certainly were all the rage. It was, in fact, their national popularity that led to the belief that they originated from the French court, but the following romantic story tells how they most probably found their way into royal circles.

Apparently, in 1390, Charles VI was mentally disturbed, so to divert his attention from terrible bouts of depression, not to mention obsession, Odette, his lovely and attentive mistress, would sing, play the harp and read to him. Always searching for new pastimes, she heard that in Paris there was talk of an exciting new game, brought to the city by gypsies. This game consisted of strange cards, some of which were numbered and others covered with pictures of eastern kings and queens which, when arranged in various combinations created amusement that amazed the players. Wishing above all else to maintain the King's favour, Odette sent for a set of these cards, but before she let him see them she had a court artist decorate a special pack, cleverly designed by herself.

Kings, queens and knaves were easily recognized in this unique pack as none other than members of the royal court. Odette and Charles were prominent among the picture cards and it is said that at the sight of them the King recovered his mental faculty immediately, albeit temporarily, and ordered that the whole world should know about the powers and magic of the cards! From this time on, picture cards in the pack became known as court cards.

The financial accounts for the French court in 1392 show a large treasury payment for 'three packs of handmade cards'. With the King's money and influence plus Odette's talent the cards were soon launched on the royal road to success. Soon every family in Paris possessed a pack and a card-producing business prospered well, but this is not the end of the story. A gypsy heard of the King's interest in the ancient cards and made herself known to Odette, telling her that although she, Odette, knew how to amuse the King with them, she knew nothing of their powers of prophecy.

Taking the pack of royal cards in her hand, the gypsy selected twelve of them and spread these on a table before her. She then proceeded to reel off personal secrets known only to Odette and the King himself, just as if she were reading from an open book. This information related not only to the past and present but foretold future events too, which later proved to be correct.

Odette now saw the cards as an oracle and, although she was told by the gypsy to keep this aspect of them to herself, she could not resist telling an indiscreet friend about her new-found source of wisdom. In no time at all the entire court was using the cards to uncover political plots, hatch new ones and discover secret love-affairs until, in the end, the King himself was obliged to ban all cards, in and out of court, by royal edict.

Their sudden removal was not welcomed within royal circles generally and, in particular, by a famous soldier of the day named La Hire. Through the magic of the cards he had learned of a certain lady's love for him so he had every reason to be grateful to them. He was, therefore, determined to have this royal ban removed at any price. Therefore, he hatched the following devious yet clever plan to do just this.

Calling again on the court artist, he had an entirely new and different pack made. This time it depicted mythological gods and goddesses, biblical characters, historical and national heroes and three members of the present court – the King, Odette and himself. Caesar, Charlemagne, Alexander and Charles VI were the four kings whilst the four brave knaves were Hogier, Lancelot, Hector and La Hire. For the four queens he chose Pallas, the goddess of arms, Judith the great Jewess, Rachel the symbol of Ysebeau and Argine the gentle fairy, who looked remarkably like Odette.

La Hire extended this patriotic and military theme to the four suits too. Clubs he said represented the sword-guards; hearts the shape of the drawn cross-bow; diamonds the heads of the war arrows and spades the tools of the same name, necessary for digging in in times of siege. When the King saw how the new cards reflected a glorious national image of France, not to mention a touch of personal flattery, he could not refuse La Hire's earnest request that the ban should be removed. In no time at all the cards were back in favour and were spread throughout the court, Paris and France once again.

From now on the 52 cards were consulted before every military campaign as seriously as they were for *affaires de coeur*. In this respect, history tells us how, four hundred years later, Napoleon planned and won many of his battles, including the winning of the famous Josephine, through the cards' revelations. It is said that this lady was delighted when, as a comparatively minor figure at court, the cards foretold that one day she would ascend the great throne of France. Unfortunately, she did not heed the warning they also gave which said that unless she moderated her temper and controlled her moodiness once in favour with the great dictator, she would surely fall from glory. And this is exactly what happened.

Meanwhile, across the channel in England the cards were enjoying similar popularity and as early as 1463 Edward IV passed a law forbidding the importation of all foreign cards into the country. This was done not to forbid them, but solely to protect and promote the home-produced card market. Although the English king at that time was greatly in favour of the cards, the Church was all for banning them completely; but since it was within monastic walls and royal circles that they were consulted most, it stood little chance of doing this.

By the time of Elizabeth I (1558–1603) the cards were firmly established as aids to political strategy as well as a way to gain personal victory over an opponent. John Dee, Elizabeth's trusted adviser, spelled out messages from the cards which, it is said, laid the foundations for the future British Empire.

In Scotland at this time, David Rissio, Mary Queen of Scots' adviser, was revealing her future through the cards. This could hardly be called her fortune for, as a famous tapestry still in existence shows, several nasty looking spades and one small heart card revealed the worst. It is a gloomy scene with the Queen and Rissio staring in horror at the ominous message. Soon after this historical card-reading, the dreadful warning it gave came true. Mary and Rissio were both executed by order of her half-sister, Elizabeth of England.

After the reign of Elizabeth I the oracular powers of the cards were not called upon again by royalty. They were, however, still to be found in court, but their role was for amusement only. The Prince Regent in the nineteenth century held many exciting parties in London and Brighton, where playing card games for money resulted in the loss of huge country estates and entire family fortunes overnight.

The Victorian era put a stop to all this and saw the cards as distinctly evil. By then their mystical significance and oracular power for the good of the individual and mankind generally had, to all intents and purposes, vanished. The Church condemned them openly from the pulpit, describing them as the devil's invention, intended to encourage what they considered to be one of man's worst traits – gambling.

This attitude towards the cards persisted well into the twentieth century. They were still banned in many homes and most families who did have a pack never played so much as an innocent game of patience with them on Sundays. Since the

1939–45 war, attitudes have changed considerably, with a result that the original mystical purpose of the cards has once again been recognized. In this new-found enlightenment they are now consulted freely in search of guidance and warnings which will help us to steer a more harmonious and rewarding course through life.

3

THE TRADITION OF THE CARDS

A pack consists of 52 cards – 40 numbered cards and twelve court cards. These are divided into four suits – diamonds, clubs, hearts and spades. Each suit has 13 cards – an ace, two, three, four, five, six, seven, eight, nine, ten, Knave, Queen and King. There are 26 black cards and 26 red.

To distinguish these cards from the Tarot pack they are often referred to as 'ordinary playing cards', but this is precisely what they are not. 'Extraordinary' would be a far more accurate description for not only do they reflect the mysterious relationship with our surroundings, they actually symbolize, numerically, the universe on a vast time scale as well. It is this link with time, as we know it, that gives a clue as to how the cards reveal past, present and future events.

Days, Weeks, Seasons and Years

Traditionally, the 52 cards symbolize the 52 weeks in a year and the four suits represent the four seasons. There is, therefore, one card for each week of the year and one suit for each season. Just as a year is divided into four parts or seasons, so too is a day and a lifetime. Each of these quarters is ruled over by one of the four suits.

The Four Elements

Additionally, the suits symbolize the four elements of nature – air, fire, water and earth. In turn, these natural forces correspond with the basic four-fold nature within man himself. Ancient philosophers classified these characteristics as choleric, sanguine, phlegmatic and melancholic, collectively called the four humours. Today, they are better known as intuition, intelligence, compassion and depression.

The Four Suits

Each of the four suits has a unique characteristic of its own. They relate to the four seasons – spring, summer, autumn and winter; the four elements – air, fire, water and earth; the four weeks in a lunar month; the four parts of a day; the four stages in a lifetime – infancy, adolescence, adulthood and old age; and the four basic psychological characteristics – intuition, intelligence, compassion and depression.

The ace of each suit rules the first week of its corresponding season. Kings rule the second week, Queens rule the third week, Knaves rule the fourth week, tens rule the fifth week and so on, with the twos ruling the last week in each season.

The first week of a cartomancy year is 1 March to 7 March and is ruled by the first card in the pack, the ace of diamonds. The last week in this year is 22 February to 28 February and is ruled by the 2 of spades, the last and lowest card in the pack. The extra day in a leap-year is, appropriately, under the rulership of the Joker.

Duality – Red and Black Cards

Duality plays a vital role in our lives as indeed it does throughout the entire universe. Since this principle is reflected in everything we do and think it is not surprising to discover that it is the underlying principle of the cards too. This is symbolized by the colours red and black. Red cards are generally feminine with all the attributes associated with this characteristic and black cards are masculine and have correspondingly opposite attributes.

Duality is really a question of balance. Night and day, north and south, positive and negative, winter and summer, hot and cold and Yin and Yang are a few examples we take for granted. The nature kingdom also conforms to this duality, with female and male counterparts in plants, animals and man, in an effort to keep the balance. Individually, we are introduced to this principle through our relationship with our mother and father, who symbolize the feminine and masculine characteristics. As we grow older we develop positive and negative moods on a psychological level. These vary from passive, inner seeking to active, outer searching, which are the opposite ends of the scale.

When the cards are consulted specifically for a character reading, this duality is revealed through combinations of the black and red cards. Synchronistically and symbolically they are then interpreted as degrees and types of extrovert and introvert tendencies.

The 365 Days in a Year

The 365 days in a year are not forgotten either for they are found in the cards in at least two numerically disguised ways.

The first is that when any three cards are chosen they give a possible combination of seven separate meanings. For example, if the three cards in question were the ace of diamonds, 2 of diamonds and 3 of diamonds, they are assessed first individually, then in twos and finally all three together, giving a total of seven different combinations. Seven, of course, is the number of days in a week and when this number is multiplied by 52, the number of weeks in a year, the figure reached is 364. Add to this one further unit representing the pack as a whole and the significant total is 365.

Another instance in which the magic number of 365 is produced is by adding the total number of pips on all the numbered cards to the number of court cards, plus their total value, on the basis of ten for each such card, and then finally adding thirteen, the number of cards in each suit. As the following calculations show, the result is 365.

The number of pips on the 40 numbered cards	= 220
The number of court cards	= 12
The 12 court cards counted as ten each	= 120
The 13 cards in each suit	= 13
	365

The Numbers Twelve and Thirteen

The thirteen cards in each suit symbolize the thirteen lunar months in a year, the thirteen weeks in each quarter and the twelve calendar months plus the year as a whole. They also represent Jesus and His twelve Apostles, Jacob and the twelve tribes of Israel, King Arthur and his twelve knights, Robin Hood and his twelve merry men, twelve signs of the zodiac revolving around the heavens, twelve gods on Mount Olympus and last but not least, the solar system. According to ancient tradition, this originally had twelve planets, one of which was the moon, orbiting the sun.

The twelve court cards in a pack represent the twelve followers or supporters found in all religious and mythological hierarchies throughout the ages. 'The twelve days of Christmas' referred to in the carol and the significance of the twelfth-night brings this principle down to a more personal level. A recent example of this same theme is found in the popular record a few years ago called 'Deck of Cards', which describes the virtues and lessons to be learned from each card, in religious and philosophical words set to music.

The number thirteen, twelve plus one, plays an important role in astrology and astronomy, as well as in religion and mythology and, whilst there are some who regard this number as unlucky, there are others who see it as a distinctly happy and positive sign. Its negative association arose from the New Testament text concerning the twelve Apostles who sat with Jesus around the table for the Last Supper. Its positive association, on the other hand, also arose from the Bible. In the Jewish faith the thirteenth year is seen as one of fulfilment, so when a boy reaches his thirteenth birthday he is said to have come of age and reached a stage of maturity to be celebrated in a memorable way.

As a number, thirteen is therefore neither fortunate nor unfortunate; it is nevertheless of great importance, signifying a completion of one cycle and the beginning of the next. It is the death of the old yet, at the same time, the birth of the new. In the cards this special number is represented by the ace in each suit, ranking high when it follows the King. It is the first and the last card, the Alpha and Omega.

The Trinity
Sacred trinities existed in religious cults long before orthodox Christianity recognized the Holy Trinity. Known as the 'three faces of God', the Egyptians worshipped Isis, Osiris and Horus and in Celtic mythology these same three aspects were Belinis, Taranis and Hesus. In the cards this trinity pattern is represented by King, Queen and Knave in each suit.

The Number Forty
The forty numbered cards in a pack remind us of events in the Old and New Testaments. We read that the Israelites wandered for forty years in the wilderness before entering the Promised Land. Moses remained forty days on Mount Sinai and Elijah was forty days in solitude. Jesus Christ fasted for forty days in the desert. He preached for forty months and was forty hours in the tomb. Jerusalem was destroyed forty years after the Ascension.

It takes forty weeks to have a baby and it is said that forty winks is as good as a full night's sleep! St Swithin, in the ninth century, forecast rain for forty days and forty nights, if it rained on the 15 July, a day now remembered each year as St Swithin's day.

Numerically and symbolically the 52 cards form a collective backcloth in front of which we, as individuals, stand. The relationship between ourselves and our environment is on many levels; some associations we can see clearly, but others we cannot. With the cards it becomes apparent immediately we recognize their symbolic link with the universe, reflecting, as they do, the principle of 'as above, so below'. The many traditional aspects of all this are equally divided between the four suits.

Conversation and the Cards

There are many sources which enrich a language and the cards have certainly played their part so far as English speech is concerned. When we call someone a 'card' we are paying them a sort of compliment for it shows they have a hidden mystique which is both amusing and intriguing.

If a specific card, like an ace, is chosen to describe a person, then their ability and expertise is established immediately because there is only one definition of an 'ace' pilot or 'ace' driver. For that matter, there is only one meaning for a 'Joker' because everyone knows what to expect when he is around!

The 'Jack' of all trades may be master of none, but at least he is more suitable than a 'knave'! And what better advice can be given than to encourage someone to 'play their cards right'? If we feel they have a few 'aces up their sleeve' or even 'hold all the aces', so much the better for this will certainly help them 'to follow suit' when the time is right and, who knows, they may even 'win hands down'.

To say 'it's on the cards' sums it all up but often in life, as with the cards, it is not always advisable to 'show your hand' or 'lay all your cards on the table' at once. Try to keep a 'poker-face' then, especially if you want to 'come up trumps'!

Games Played with the Cards

It is said that the ancient sages gave the cards a two-fold attraction. One aspect was to appeal to man's nobler quality, his search for knowledge and wisdom, whilst the other was to pander to his lesser virtue, a pursuit of greed and amusement. If this is so, then they certainly succeeded in the last respect because card games, especially those played for money, are as popular today as they were in the days of the French court.

The majority of card games played in Britain today came originally from the Continent, although over the years these have been modified and given new names. Soldiers returning home from wars in Europe brought back most of these, notably 'Napoleon', better known as 'Nap'. And during the First World War the troops played a French game called '*vingt-et-un*' which, after slightly altering the rules, was renamed 'pontoon'.

Emigrants to the U.S.A. took the cards with them, and from the smoky saloons dotted along the highways to the West emerged that well known gambling game, 'poker'. This again was an adaptation of a French bluffing game called '*poque*', hence the importance of the 'poker-face'. The States later gave birth to 'gin rummy' and 'slippery sam' and with the samba in the 1960s came the latest edition of all, 'canasta'. This belongs to the rummy family.

A typical English card game is 'cribbage', played with cards, a board and pegs. This is said to have been invented by Sir John Suckling a famous gambler of the seventeenth century. More recently, 'Newmarket', named after the racing town in East Anglia, has become very popular in family circles, where only small bets of a few pence or even buttons are at stake.

On a more sober note we have 'bridge' and 'whist'. Bridge parties and whist drives are held regularly in homes and church halls up and down the country. Here, they rarely play for money, but prizes are nevertheless given and although the players would be loath to call it gambling, they still compete pretty fiercely in order to win!

This is by no means a complete list of card games but last and not least we have the solo game of 'patience'. This is said to have been played in French bistros by artists whiling away their time over a glass of wine, testing both the patience of *le patron* and themselves.

The Name of the Game

When remembering that the other purpose of the cards was to reveal our mysterious relationship with our surroundings, it is not surprising that even a game of cards symbolizes the game of life itself. This aspect is the opposite side of the coin from that of gambling and amusement, but is always present.

Take any game of cards you like, gambling or otherwise. After a hand is dealt the players look at the cards to see what they have. Some of these will be good, others will be bad and the rest mediocre. Compare this hand with personal attributes and handicaps, assets and liabilities, credits and deficits and joys and sorrows dealt to us by the hand of Fate. When a good hand is dealt to a player in a card game, it appears that he has an advantage from the start; so too it would seem that the person born with every luxury, good looks and good health, is on to a winning streak. Should both players make the most of what they have, then the chances are they will both succeed. But if they fail to make the right moves at the right time and generally play their cards badly, then they will undoubtedly end up the losers.

On the other hand, players who receive appalling cards, like people born into deprived circumstances, may play what cards they have extremely well and, purely through their own efforts and determination, turn out to win hands down! The lesson to be learned from this is that by making the best of what we have been dealt, whether they are cards in a pretend game or opportunities in the real game of life, we can still win in the end.

4

DIVINATION AND THE CARDS

At one time the observation of virtually everything provided grounds for divination. The clouds – nephelmancy; the winds – austromancy; smoke – capnomancy; a flight of birds – ornithomancy; the flame from a lamp – lampadomancy and the water from a fountain – pegomancy; these were all sources for potential forecasting. The throwing of rice onto a flat surface, tea–leaves left in a cup and pictures in the fire also created signs to be interpreted as omens but, in each case, it was the abstract shapes formed by these that served to awaken the intuitive powers of the interpreters.

The cards are also omens but they are something more than symbolic patterns which depend on the psychic ability of the interpreter for interpretation. Down the ages the four suits have inherited definite characteristics and meanings which are basically constant and each card represents a different aspect of the suit to which it belongs. Intuition, so far as the cards are concerned, comes into play mainly in the interpretation of the symbolic, over–all message which links up with personal circumstances.

Synchronicity – Coincidence and Chance
There is undoubtedly a connection between the human psyche and external events, the inner and outer worlds. All religions teach the existence of an underlying link between ourselves and others and with the universe as a whole. Explanations concerning this vary considerably and none are really convincing, nor are they complete within themselves.

Synchronicity, defined by C. G. Jung as 'a meaningful coincidence', is one way in which this connection manifests itself in our daily lives. More often than not such moments usually pass by unnoticed and nearly always unrecognized for what they are. The concept of synchronicity gives us an insight into just how the cards serve as a bridge or link between the inner and outer worlds. It shows that what may appear to be a coincidence or chance is, in fact, a directly related event.

But this event is not by way of the usual chain of cause and effect, action and reaction, so it cannot be traced back and explained in logical terms or in chronological order. This is because the synchronistic event does not arise from linear time but from that 'out-of-time moment', the 'eternal now'.

The English language has only one word for time but the ancients, in particular the Greeks, had two – *kronos* and *kairos*. These describe the difference between the experience of time and the quality of time. *Kronos,* also spelt *chronos,* is measured time as we know it, giving us experiences in chronological order. *Kairos,* sometimes spelt *cairos,* giving us the link with Egypt, is participation within time itself and gives us timeless-ness. It is during moments of *kairos* that synchronistic events occur, showing we are 'at one with' and not 'separate from' our surroundings.

Oracles and Jung

Having found that humanity was motivated by inner creative instincts as well as outer material drives, Jung began to investigate the unseen synchronistic link between us and our surroundings. This led him to the *I Ching,* otherwise known as *The Book of Changes.* The *I Ching* is considered to be an oracle in book form and is consulted in exactly the same way as the cards. Messages in this book, like those written into the cards, are symbolic, so before they can be understood they have to be interpreted.

Jung found that when we consult an oracle such as the cards, the *I Ching* or any other form of divination for that matter, we are deliberatly attempting to produce a reading through synchronicity. We are, by virtue of unconsciously selecting certain cards, putting ourselves into a position whereby we actually cause that coinciding or synchronistic moment of *kairos* – timelessness. The result of this is that we contact the past, present and future.

5

HOW TO CONSULT THE CARDS

A successful reading depends on a truly representative selection of cards chosen by the questioner and the ability of the interpreter to understand them. The questioner and the interpreter may be one and the same person because we most certainly can read our own cards, but an assistant will always give a much more objective assessment of the situation.

The first qualification necessary to become a good cartomancer is a genuine desire to do so! This, backed up with plenty of enthusiasm and lots of practice is all that is needed to succeed. If there is a 'feeling' for the cards then so much the better. Although meanings of individual cards are readily available, it is the intuitive association and linking together of these that gives depth to the over-all message. A psychic and sensitive nature is an advantage, but this is something that actually develops through working with the cards in their oracular capacity.

When first learning to read the cards use nothing more than their basic meanings. This will give an over-all message and assessment of a situation although it may appear somewhat stilted. Remembering that 'practice makes perfect', confidence is soon gained and the intuitive links between one card and another quickly develop.

The most difficult part of an interpretation is telling the questioner that obstacles are ahead, especially when that person is already in trouble. It helps to know that by doing this you are helping them to avoid a problem or, at the very least, saving them from being taken by complete surprise. It is essential that you offer hope where there is despair and give comfort in place of sorrow. Look for a solution, which can always be seen in the cards alongside the problem, rather like the healing dock being found next to the spiteful nettle. Again, practice is necessary to recognize these symbolic antidotes among the hurdles.

Traditional Rituals

There are traditional rituals involved in selecting and reading the cards which should be observed wherever possible. This helps to bring into play those synchronistic moments which allow the questioner, unconsciously, to select the right cards. It also increases the awareness of the interpreter and generally produces harmony between them and the cards.

Ideally, a new pack of cards should be purchased and kept solely for the purpose of divination. These should be handled only by yourself and questioners who select spreads from them for you to interpret. No games of any nature should ever be played with them.

Cards for divination should really be kept in a set place, preferably higher than table-top level. It is said this keeps them above mundane matters and the best place is the top shelf of a dark cupboard. True initiates of the cards advocate that a hand-sewn silk bag is made for them to which they are returned immediately after a reading. This is done to preserve their oracular power which increases with proper use. Mishandling and using them for card games releases this energy with a result that their harmonies are disturbed, affecting both questioner and interpreter.

The Questioner and Interpreter

Before a spread can be chosen, questioners must decide whether they want a general reading or one that highlights a particular aspect of their life. If, for example, their concern is their love life then a spread suitable for this would be very different from one designed to give an over-all picture of their situation. Again, if a character analysis is required yet another spread would be preferred. The number of questions asked from a spread does not matter, although three is usual, so long as they relate to the subject in question.

It will also be necessary to choose a representative court card for some of the spreads. The secret of discovering the most appropriate one lies in assessing a personal standpoint in relation to a problem or situation, as described later in 'How to Choose a Court Card'.

Preparation for a Reading

Handling the cards is most important for it imprints them with personal vibrations. Before using new cards for a reading, shuffle and cut them as many times as possible and, whilst doing so, look closely at their intricate designs and numbers. The more you familiarize yourself with these the better they respond to your questions.

A relaxed atmosphere is essential when reading the cards. The burning of a joss-stick helps achieve this and so does a warm room rather than a cold one. From a purely practical point of view make sure that the table is large enough to accommodate the spread because if it is bunched up, continuity and expansion of thought are correspondingly hampered. If possible use a round table and then sit with your back to the North and have the questioner facing you with their back to the South.

Procedure

Before placing the pack of cards on the table the interpreter must shuffle them to rid them of any previous influence. If a court card is necessary to represent the questioner it is chosen at this stage, after the initial shuffling by the interpreter. Having decided on this it is then carefully placed to one side, ready to be included in the final selection.

The remaining 51 cards, or 52 cards if a court card is not necessary, are now handed to the questioner who, with the nature of their problem or situation clearly and uppermost in their mind, proceeds to shuffle them thoroughly. The cards are then ceremoniously placed in the centre of the table and are cut by the questioner three times with the left hand. (This hand is nearer the heart, both anatomically and emotionally).

Next, the interpreter picks them up and spreads them face downwards across the table, in a slightly overlapping line. They are now ready for the questioner to make a selection, the number of which will depend on the spread chosen for the reading. This selection is done completely spontaneously when it will be found that the eye leads the hand, the left hand, automatically to certain cards. As they are chosen they are removed and placed face downwards in a small pack, strictly in order of choice. When the required number has been extracted the remaining cards should be removed from the table.

Placing the Court Card

If the spread requires a personal court card it is added by the questioner now. Keeping the selected cards face downwards so that their values are not revealed, the personal card is placed among them. This may be a random placing or a calculated, conscious decision as to where it is inserted; it may be exactly in the middle, the third, the ninth, the fifth position etc. This choice is entirely up to the questioner.

The interpreter now takes the selected cards, with or without the personal court card, in readiness to arrange them into a particular spread. At this point it may be necessary to turn the cards over so that the bottom card, the first one chosen, is at the top. This is most important if the cards are to be placed in order of selection.

When a satisfactory reading has been completed the cards are reunited into a full pack and thoroughly shuffled by the interpreter in order to disconnect them from present association. They are then returned to their secluded place of safety in readiness for the next reading.

6

HOW TO CHOOSE A COURT CARD

It is generally supposed that a fair person is represented by a red King, Queen or Jack and a dark person by one of the black court cards. For readings of an over-all nature, covering every aspect of life this basic representation is sufficient, but for a specialized reading, focussing on a particular aspect or problem, a much more characteristic court card is needed. After all, appearance, like beauty, is only skin-deep.

We have, within each of us, the four characteristics symbolized by the four suits. These are proportionately different in every individual and although it may appear that some people are typical diamonds and have no heart, they nevertheless possess this aspect along with the other two, hidden away somewhere. Even the most rigid types have to show their hand sometimes and it is the ability to do this at the right time that makes for a more balanced existence.

Life demands that we play different roles to suit different occasions, so automatically most of us are able to adapt and act the part. An excellent example of this change of role is the hard-headed King of diamonds who falls madly in love and becomes the compassionate King of hearts overnight! But should our work or career be at stake, then our King, Queen or Jack of hearts image is not the one to wear at such times; it is the King, Queen or Jack of diamonds-self who best represents this standpoint; and when money matters are pressing, the King, Queen or Jack of clubs must be 'top dog' then.

In the past, divorced people have always been portrayed by the King or Queen of spades. Unless these are particularly bitter and twisted about their position, these cards are a total misrepresentation and in no way represent them. It is usual for a Queen court card to represent a woman, a King court card to represent a mature man and a Jack court card to represent a younger man. In these days of equality of the sexes, with equal pay for equal work, it may be more appropriate in some cases for a woman to choose a King or a Jack court card and a man to choose a Queen. As time changes, society alters its standpoint;

and so, too, do the cards; therefore, from the following descriptions choose the one which best represents you in relation to your looks, problem situation or question.

A Court Card for General Readings

Decide on your outer appearance for these readings and then choose the court card which describes you best.

Diamond Court Cards represent very fair people with flaxen, light red or white hair, light blue or green eyes and a very pale complexion. Slim Nordic types are true diamonds.

Heart Court Cards represent fair people too, but those with slightly richer coloured hair and complexions than diamond types. They have blue, grey or hazel eyes and light brown or auburn hair. Plump, family people are often typical hearts.

Club Court Cards represent those with rich brown hair, brown eyes and colourful complexions. Energetic Latin races are generally club types.

Spade Court Cards represent very dark-skinned people with raven black hair and dark eyes. They always have plenty of energy in reserve and are physically strong.

A Court Card for Specialized Readings

Choosing the right court card for these readings depends entirely on the personal standpoint in relation to a problem, situation or question and has nothing whatsoever to do with outer appearance. Select the most appropriate from the suits below.

Diamond Court Cards represent those concerned with practical matters relating to work, career, promotion, redundancy, ambitions, aims, property, moves, travel and all forms of communication including acting, writing and artistic painting. Efficient, practical people and those who think mainly with their heads, such as professional and business people and manual workers are these diamond types.

Heart Court Cards represent those who are facing emotional problems, romantic entanglements, marriage and heartfelt relationships. All who think with their hearts and the love-lorn are heart types, so too are family-minded people.

Club Court Cards represent those with financial interests and problems involving investments, deals, gifts, monetary surprises, debts and bankruptcy. Bank managers, budding tycoons, misers and paupers are club types.

Spade Court Cards represent those who feel hope is fading fast. They may be in a terrible state facing court cases, worried about a health problem and generally surrounded by negative circumstances. The unfortunate person, albeit temporarily, is the spade type. So, too, are judges, lawyers and all who wield authority.

A Court Card for Psychic Readings

Your standpoint is very important and in this respect it depends mainly on whether you have a positive or negative psychic nature and how long you have been involved with psychism, occultism and philosophy.

Diamond Court Cards represent positive psychics including clairvoyants, astrologers, cartomancers, occultists and healers. If a newcomer to these arts, then choose a diamond court card.

Heart Court Cards represent negative-receptive psychics including mediums, inspirational speakers, intuitive workers and healers.

Club Court Cards represent experienced psychics and those who have returned to the scene after a break for some reason. They may be either positive or negative psychics or a mixture of both.

Spade Court Cards represent those who work entirely alone and not with a group. They are lone workers and seekers but are not necessarily advanced in their understanding. Often they cannot tell the difference between the right and wrong occult path.

A Court Card for a Character Reading

This card should reflect what you consider to be your more permanent personality and not a transient mood of the moment. Find yourself in the suits below and choose accordingly.

Diamond Court Cards represent hopeful positive people with plenty of good ideas and untapped mental resources. They are generally outward-looking and extrovert by nature.

Heart Court Cards represent emotional people capable of great depths of feeling. They are sometimes over-sensitive and compassionate, inward-looking and introvert by nature.

Club Court Cards represent determined people who seek external riches and support from others to gain confidence. They think with both their head and their heart.

Spade Court Cards represent those who see life as a dark, hopeless battle. Most of the time they are depressed and look too closely at themselves and the underlying meaning of life.

7

HOW TO CHOOSE A SPREAD

There are many spreads from which to choose and these are based either on the British system, which uses 52 cards or on the Continental system, which uses only 32 cards. Since the Continental system means discarding all cards below number seven, except the four aces, a reading is bound to give an incomplete assessment of a situation. Simply because a card is numerically low it does not follow that its symbolic significance is correspondingly low. In addition to this, the removal of these so-called lower cards completely destroys the cosmic significance, numerically reflecting the principle of 'as above, so below'.

All numbers are equally important and the number two, missing from Continental spreads, is just one example. This number introduces into the suits questions of duality, opposition, partnership, harmony, disharmony, balance and counterbalance, the basis, in fact, of life itself. When choosing a traditionally Continental method I therefore suggest that cards are selected from a full 52-card pack and not from a watered down version containing only 32 cards.

Continental spreads also distinguish between upright and reversed meanings of a card. This can introduce unnecessary complications into a reading, mainly because foreign authorities vary in their interpretation. Nevertheless, most sources agree that a reversal gives a definitely gloomy meaning even to the most positive and encouraging cards!

Upright and reversed cards belong strictly to the tarot pack where different meanings are clear and important. If this added aspect is desired and your cards are not designed to show which way up they are, then mark them yourself with a 'U' and an 'R' to give them a top and a bottom. British cards do not usually indicate this, except in the cases of the ace of hearts, the ace of clubs and the ace of spades. This is not through design but because their shapes are not symmetrical. The meanings of reversed cards, according to one French source, are given along with the other definitions of individual cards.

A spread represents a situation, problem or question which the suits reflect symbolically on a practical, psychological and psychic level. Each of the 52 cards indicates an event, a quality, a characteristic and an influence and, depending on the spread used, these will be brought to life through the meaning of each card and those surrounding it. For example, the 7 of diamonds on the practical level symbolizes personal ambitions, aims and materialistic plans for the future, but only neighbouring cards will tell us the likelihood of success or failure. Alone, the meaning of this card remains a bare statement of fact.

From the following seven spreads choose the one most likely to reflect your problem, situation or questions. Remember, they symbolize conditions and give symbolic answers which then have to be interpreted on the appropriate level as we are back again to the importance of the personal, fundamental standpoint. Establish this and the rest is easy.

8

THE MYSTICAL CROSS

This is a British spread originating from the Knights Templars. It gives us an excellent over-all assessment of a personal situation on all levels, indicating relationships between lovers, family, friends and acquaintances, career and business prospects, ambitions, money matters and the inevitable obstacles and hurdles in life too. It also shows individual characteristics and psychic potential so may also be used for a character study or psychic reading.

Method
A personal court card is necessary to represent the questioner, plus twelve more, making thirteen cards in all. Having carried out the ritualistic preparation and chosen the most appropriate court card, remove this from the pack. The remaining 51 cards are then spread face downwards across the table in a slightly overlapping line, by the interpreter. Twelve cards are selected from these by the questioner, who keeps them strictly in the order of selection. The court card is then placed significantly among them in the way previously described.

The interpreter now takes the thirteen cards and turns them face upwards, thus revealing the first card selected, and arranges them to form the equilateral cross as shown in Diagram 1 (on page 38).

The line down represents the present situation and the line across reflects influences which will affect this situation. The position of the court card is noted first. If this is in the line down, it shows the questioner's circumstances are likely to control them more than they are able to control their circumstances. If it is in the line across, then it means it is well within their power to control and influence matters. Should this court card be in the middle of the cross then the questioner is assured that the situation will shortly be resolved in a most satisfactory way.

The card in the centre of the cross is interpreted next. This indicates the major aspect around which everything revolves at present. It is both a cause and an effect, with its significance depending on the suit and individual meaning of the card.

Cards in the line down are interpreted individually and linked together to symbolize aspects of the present situation. Finally, the cards in the line across are interpreted individually as influences which will alter the present situation in the future.

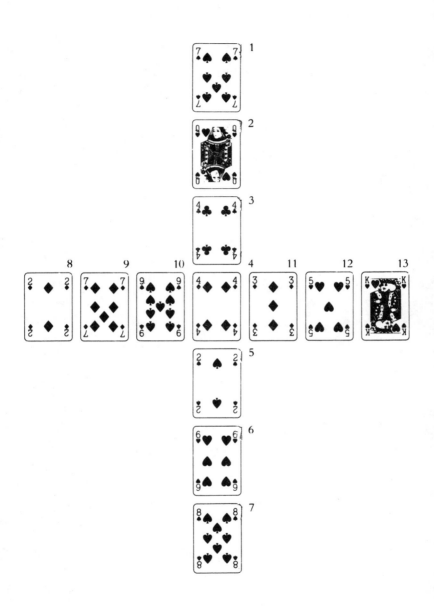

Diagram 1

The Mystical Cross

THE MYSTICAL CROSS

7 of spades

Queen of hearts

4 of clubs

2 of diamonds/7 of diamonds/9 of spades/4 of diamonds/3 of diamonds/5 of hearts/King of hearts

2 of spades

6 of hearts

8 of spades

Question: What does the future hold for me?

Court Card: Queen of hearts

Combinations and Relationships of the Cards:

Two Twos: Separate ways

Two Fours: Uncertainty at present

Two Sevens: Mutual Love

Position of the Court Card: This is in the line down showing that circumstances control the questioner more than she is able to control them.

The line down represents the present situation.

7 of Spades: The fact that this card heads this line indicates that personal fears and worries dominate the situation. Most of these will come to nothing but, even so, a shadow is cast over everything, producing apprehension and negativity.

Queen of Hearts: This court card represents the questioner. Her family, home and emotional happiness are her life. There seem to be worries on the one hand, 7 of spades, and money troubles on the other, 4 of clubs. 'Thinking' mainly with her heart, not her head, neither of these problems will be easily resolved.

4 of Clubs: This card warns of the loss of an asset. It might be a purse, key or other valuable personal possession but, at the same time, it also indicates difficulties to make ends meet financially.

4 of Diamonds: Much revolves around this card because it is in the centre of the cross. Practical problems are difficult to solve and communications with others seem to break down. Decision making is virtually impossible so this prolongs the issue.

2 of Spades: Two sides of the question are seen but both look equally bad. The practical decision reflected in the previous card comes to a head and steps will have to be taken soon.

6 of Hearts: Again, two sets of circumstances are at loggerheads. A compromise is going to be the only way out and this will entail considerable self-sacrifice, emotionally.

8 of Spades: A drain on resources brings depression and lack of energy. It is advisable that the questioner trusts no one but herself. Health must be watched carefully.

The line across reflects influences which will affect the present situation.

2 of Diamonds: This dual influence will help solve the situation in a very practical way, but its value is not recognized at the time.

7 of Diamonds: This influence represents the questioner's practical plans and initiative which, until now, seems to have been sadly lacking. Once this begins to develop, she can expect action. Self-confidence will grow from this point.

9 of Spades: Depressing though this influence is, at least it brings action. By seeing it as a necessary evil the questioner should know that the present is a stage which must be passed through before better times are reached.

4 of Diamonds: As an influence, this card emphasizes loyalties which conflict with what should be done. The head must rule over the heart in this instance.

3 of Diamonds: Practical drive and enthusiasm will develop with this influence. Determination, so necessary to get out of the present rut, will also emerge.

5 of Hearts: A decision to escape from the real issue is felt with this influence. Personal feelings will be overruled by the practical scene, but this is the only way out of a negative situation.

King of Hearts: It can only be assumed that this King represents the questioner's husband. If this is so, then he too is a 'heart-thinker' so is little help in producing a practical solution to his wife's problem. It is, however, a compassionate influence which no doubt gives plenty of comfort and love to her.

Conclusions: The present situation, symbolized by the cards, shows life is getting this person down. Much of her trouble is looking too closely and intently at herself in relation to circumstances. An unknowing selfishness exists which would vanish if she took a different view point of the whole scene.

Future influences help solve all this but the cards also point out that she needs to adopt a more practical approach to life in order to balance the emotional outlook she has at present.

9

THE HORSESHOE OF FATE

The 'horseshoe of fate' originated from the gypsies who took it to France from the Middle East many centuries ago. It is both a simple and effective method, appropriate for a specialized reading relating to all heartfelt problems, changes in work, moving house, travel and money matters.

Method

Seven cards are selected by the questioner, in the ritualistic manner, from the full pack. No court card is needed. These seven cards are then handed to the interpreter who turns them over to reveal the first card selected, and then sets them out in the order shown in Diagram 2 (on page 42).

Card number 1 represents past influences contributing to the present situation. *Card number 2* reveals choices and alternatives. *Card number 3* represents stability or instability. *Card number 4* shows cross-currents, influences and challenges. *Card number 5* shows openings or obstacles. *Card number 6* tells who or what your friends or foes are and *card number 7* indicates the final outcome.

This spread is interpreted through the individual meanings of the cards which are then applied to personal circumstances.

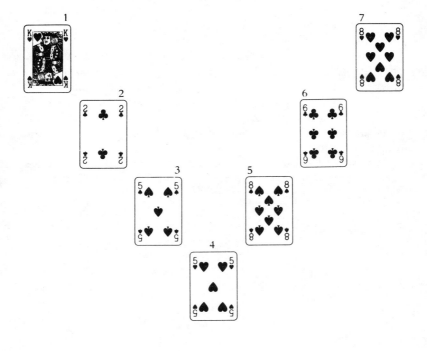

Diagram 2

The Horseshoe of Fate

THE HORSESHOE OF FATE

King of hearts	8 of hearts
2 of clubs	6 of clubs
5 of spades	8 of spades
5 of hearts	

Question: Will I win the personal battle arising from business affairs and money complications?

Combinations and Relationships of the Cards:

Two Fives: Personal uncertainty

Two Eights: Inconstancy

Card Number 1: Past influences contributing to the present situation.

King of Hearts: This card reflects the questioner's own character and influence, revealing he has a pretty easy-going nature. In the past he has let others take an unfair advantage of him. Although usually of persuasive nature, this applies more to emotional situations than to business, so in this respect he would be relatively powerless. Much of the present trouble arises from this and amounts almost to neglect of practical matters.

Card Number 2: Choice and alternatives.

2 of Clubs: A change is inevitable but making a choice in conjunction with this is going to be rather difficult because there is not much to choose from. Opposition delays things and money will be the issue. Seeing things from another point of view will help, but beware of an 'out of the frying pan and into the fire' situation developing.

Card Number 3: Stability or instability.

5 of Spades: Troubles are undoubtedly causing insecurity leading to some degree of instability. Complications prolong things but there is one aspect which offers hope for the future; set-backs will be followed by eventual success so despondency is warned against.

Card Number 4: Cross-current challenges and influences.

5 of Hearts: This represents personal reactions to the situation. Inner feelings from the heart are very different from the logic of the head. There is a desire to escape from these emotions but they are part of the battle or challenge. The tendency is to bury the head in the sand so courage is necessary to overcome these personal feelings.

Card Number 5: Opportunities or obstacles.

8 of Spades: A definite obstacle must be faced before moving on to more fulfilling circumstances. False friends are warned against, too. Despondency, with the added problem of depression, become obstacles in themselves so try to keep these in perspective.

Card Number 6: Friends or foes.

6 of Clubs: Help will be forthcoming from a most unexpected source. In this way, friends will prove themselves by giving practical or financial assistance. There are many ways in which they might do this, even as a last minute rescue operation.

Card Number 7: The final outcome.

8 of Hearts: Although the present seems to be in a turmoil, there are hopes for much happier times. A new-found satisfaction is indicated by this card, provided the right cards are played at the right time. In other words, by facing up to obstacles, life will be seen from a fresh standpoint, with new light falling on old, dark situations. In this way, the battle will be won.

Conclusion: In answer to the question, it appears that the outcome depends mainly on a personal, inner battle being won first. Having let things slide in the past, everything has caught up with the questioner so he must take action now to begin to put matters right. A change is coming and when true friends have been sorted out from the false, it will be possible to accept reliable and sincere help. Although an outright win is not seen in these cards, peace of mind will return eventually.

10

THE PYRAMID

Not surprisingly, this spread finds its origin in Egypt. The longer one ponders upon its message, the more it reveals and so in this we see reflections of the great pyramid itself. It is an excellent spread to symbolize a particular aspect of life, but may be used for a concise general reading too.

Method

No court card is needed. Ten cards are selected by the questioner in the true ritualistic manner and handed to the interpreter who turns them over to reveal the first card selected. This card is placed at the top of the pyramid and the others, in sequence, form the lines below, as shown in Diagram 3 (on page 46).

The card on the top line symbolizes the over-all aspect and influence affecting the problem, situation or question. *The second line* shows choice of action. *The third line* reveals underlying forces at work and the degree of stability, and *the base line* tells the questioner how they should play their cards in the future.

Diagram 3
The Pyramid

THE PYRAMID

9 of hearts

8 of clubs   5 of hearts

3 of spades   Queen of diamonds   Queen of clubs

Ace of diamonds   3 of hearts   4 of spades   6 of hearts

Question: How will my love-life work out?

Combinations and Relationships of the Cards:

Two Threes: A choice must be made

Two Queens: Curiosity

Top Card: Over-all aspect and influence.

9 of Hearts: This is the 'wish' or the 'heart's desire' card so it is no secret that this questioner has romance on his mind. It is also the most fortunate card in the pack, offering happiness and fulfilment so long as careful planning is made and put into operation.

Second Line: Choice of action.

8 of Clubs and 5 of Hearts: The alternatives are to take a chance as suggested by the 8 of clubs, the gambler's card, or not to face up to emotional feelings and responsibilities as shown by the 5 of hearts. Neither are strong decisions nor solutions which would greatly alter the present situation.

Third Line: Underlying forces producing stability or instability.

3 of Spades, Queen of Diamonds and the Queen of Clubs: This seems to reflect a two-to-one chance against a stable situation. The eternal triangle from the 3 of spades, a practical woman in the form of the Queen of diamonds and a determined woman in the Queen of clubs, together put the questioner to the spot.

Base Line: How to play one's cards best.

Ace of Diamonds, 3 of Hearts, 4 of Spades and 6 of Hearts: First of all, practical plans should be made for the future, as stressed by the ace of diamonds. Then, emotional stability, symbolized by the 3 of hearts, should be carefully considered. This is essential before the true heart's desire can be pursued properly. The 4 of spades warns against obstacles, delays and minor upsets and the 6 of hearts makes it quite clear that self-sacrifice is going to be necessary before happiness and peace of mind are found.

Conclusion: There seems to be little doubt that this gentleman is stringing along two ladies at the same time. He must make up his mind and make the choice himself. Although nothing disasterous is going to happen to him, it is hardly fair to keep both ladies in suspense.

11

THE ROMANY WAY

This spread originated from the Balkans and is used extensively by the Romany folk today, in Britain and on the Continent. Most appropriately, it reveals secrets of the heart's desires and all personal problems concerning health and wealth.

Method
No court card is needed. Twenty-one cards are selected in the true ritualistic manner by the questioner. These are handed to the interpreter who turns them over to make sure that the first card selected comes to the top. They are then arranged in sequence, as shown in Diagram 4 (on page 49).

The top line represents the past: *the middle line* represents the present; and *the bottom line* represents the future. The cards are interpreted from left to right beginning with the top line.

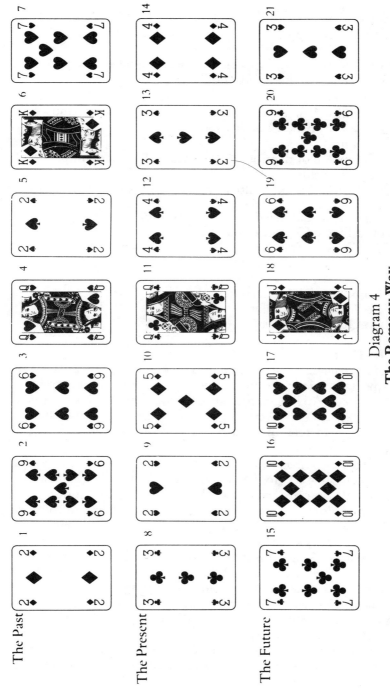

Diagram 4
The Romany Way

THE ROMANY WAY
The Past
2 of diamonds/9 of spades/6 of hearts/Queen of hearts/2 of
spades/King of diamonds/7 of hearts
The Present
3 of clubs/2 of hearts/5 of diamonds/Queen of clubs/4 of
spades/3 of spades/4 of diamonds
The Future
7 of clubs/10 of diamonds/10 of hearts/Jack of diamonds/6 of
spades/9 of clubs/3 of hearts
Question: Will I be healthy, wealthy, happy and wise in the
future?
Combinations and Relationships of the Cards:
Three Twos: Change of direction
Three Threes: Stability
Two Sixes: Contradictions
Two Sevens: Mutual love
Two Nines: Eventual contentment
Two Tens: Repayments
Two Queens: Curiosity

The Past

2 of Diamonds: A partnership on a practical basis once played an
important role in producing the stability enjoyed at present.

9 of Spades: An illness, probably followed by depression, made
a considerable impact at the time. Plans had to be altered,
especially in relation to a career and this brought great disappointment.

6 of Hearts: Through the set-back seen in the previous card a
personal self-sacrifice had to be made. This looked grim at the
time, but later proved to have been a blessing in disguise.

Queen of Hearts: A good-hearted person gave help and comfort
during those times of stress and was most likely to have been
the questioner's mother.

2 of Spades: A difficult decision had to be made and it came at
the worst possible time. Opposition and complications must
have brought further depression through the delay.

King of Diamonds: This man gave practical help and advice
which helped solve many of the difficulties. He was probably
the questioner's father.

7 of Hearts: This shows that the questioner found security
within himself during, or as a result of, those dark days. His

family stood by him and helped in every possible way.

The Present

3 of Clubs: Financial stability gives confidence and security. Progress from now on will be slow but sure and wealth in other ways will begin to accumulate.

2 of Hearts: This shows that an emotional harmonious partnership exists, where successes and heartaches are shared equally. The future will continue to be shared in this balanced way, ensuring family happiness for some time to come.

5 of Diamonds: There are thoughts and discussions concerning property and a possible move, but this is only in the air at present.

Queen of Clubs: Here is a valuable lady who must surely be the questioner's wife. Excellent when it comes to spending money, she has the gift of always making a little go a long way.

4 of Spades: Delays and minor upsets hinder plans for the future. There are difficulties in trying to please everyone, mainly because there are many sides to be considered.

3 of Spades: There seems to be a run of negativity which brings depression and uncertainty. A third person may be interfering and unbalancing everything generally.

4 of Diamonds: It is important that a practical conclusion is reached soon. This should be settled with the head and not too much help from the heart.

The Future

7 of Clubs: Thanks to careful planning in the past there is security in the future. Money will not be a worry and although great financial wealth is not foreseen, there will certainly be sufficient to meet every need.

10 of Diamonds: This indicates the end of one cycle and the beginning of the next. Retirement is on the cards and following this an interesting new life opens up. A move of house is likely at this stage.

10 of Hearts: Having started on a new practical trail, expect this to be accompanied by an equally interesting emotional outlook. Family and friends help to make up this harmony.

Jack of Diamonds: Here is a younger member of the family who gives reliable help when it is most needed. He adds vitality to life and will always be around when most needed.

6 of Spades: A disappointment is to be expected which will overshadow the peace and quiet for a while. This worry could relate to a health problem, but things soon right themselves.

9 of Clubs: Wealth, in every sense of the word, can confidently be expected. Recovery from a set-back seen in the previous card is assured and peace of mind will return.

3 of Hearts: Emotional stability and inner harmony symbolized by this card are the best gifts to bestow on any future.

Conclusion: From disappointments in the past this questioner has learned the lessons of life the hard way. Having fought and won personal battles early on gave him confidence and security. His health has improved over the years and no serious problems are foreseen in this direction. Financially, funds will be just about adequate to provide for necessities, but a wealth of understanding seems to have developed which is worth a lot more than money in the bank. There appears to be a particular problem at the moment, but this will be solved soon and will in no way spoil plans for the future.

12

THE MAGIC SQUARE

This spread was the inspiration of an ancient sage who inherited secrets from the East and the West. As you will see, it is based more on individual potential than on past, present and future events so is ideal for revealing characteristic traits and psychic abilities.

Method

A personal court card is needed to represent the questioner in relation to a character analysis or psychic reading. Having chosen this, it is placed to one side whilst the questioner shuffles the cards. With the pack remaining face downwards, cards are taken from the top by the interpreter, who places them in the order shown in Diagram 5 (on page 54).

The first four cards are taken in order from the pack and placed accordingly. The fifth card is the personal court card, and is placed over square five. The sixth, seventh, eighth and ninth cards are then taken in sequence from the pack to complete the diagram.

Each card relates to the meaning of the square it covers, and is interpreted in relation to this.

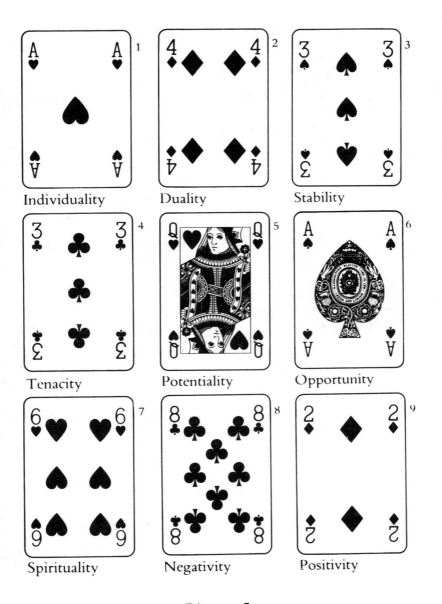

Individuality   Duality   Stability

Tenacity   Potentiality   Opportunity

Spirituality   Negativity   Positivity

Diagram 5
The Magic Square

THE MAGIC SQUARE

1	2	3
Individuality	*Duality*	*Stability*
Ace of hearts	4 of diamonds	3 of spades
4	5	6
Tenacity	*Potentiality*	*Opportunity*
3 of clubs	Queen of hearts	Ace of spades
7	8	9
Spirituality	*Negativity*	*Positivity*
6 of hearts	8 of clubs	2 of diamonds

Psychological Reading
Court Card: Queen of hearts
Combinations and Relationships of the Cards:
Two Aces: Reunion
Two Threes: Choice

Square 1 – Individuality: Ace of Hearts
There is no doubt that this lady's heart rules her head. This means her personality is distinctly one-sided and shows she assesses all situations and circumstances from an emotional standpoint. Steps should be taken to develop a more practical approach not only to problems but to life as a whole.

Square 2 – Duality: 4 of Diamonds
This card in relation to this square means there is a strong desire to become an extrovert, but the lady's very nature forbids this. As a duality, these two characteristics attempt to negate each other with a result that a nullity of personality develops.

Square 3 – Stability: 3 of Spades
Mental stability is overshadowed by a form of laziness which prevents true self-expression. Initiative and drive are needed to redress the balance, but first there must be a desire for creativity in a practical way.

Square 4 – Tenacity: 3 of Clubs
A high reserve of mental energy helps to keep up morale and pressure when faced with a battle of wits. Self-confidence will

grow from small successes and with the natural characteristic of perseverance these will grow in size and number.

Square 5 – Potentiality: Queen of Hearts
Having selected this queen as her court card it shows the questioner is an introverted lady who needs many more out-side interests. She should beware of self-pity and try not to be too sensitive. She should also try to cultivate the characteristics symbolized by the other queens since the Queen of diamonds represents practicality, the Queen of clubs represents con-fidence and the Queen of spades represents aggression. Just a little of the last queen's characteristic is all that is needed!

Square 6 – Opportunity: Ace of Spades
Unfortunately, this lady is unable to make the most of her opportunities because of a mental hang-up. Whilst she is battl-ing with inner personal turmoil the chance of extrovert self-expression is lost.

Square 7 – Spirituality: 6 of Hearts
Inner peace has not yet been found. Self-realization is desired but at the same time it is feared. Before this state can be reached a degree of self-sacrifice is necessary, involving a change of outlook.

Square 8 – Negativity: 8 of Clubs
Too much self-assessment has produced a negative person-ality. This is not only a waste of time but more often than not it comes to the wrong conclusion anyway. This situation could, however, be reversed by taking an objective view instead of a subjective one.

Square 9 – Positivity: 2 of Diamonds
Although there is a deep desire to become positive and active outwardly, attention is too divided at present to do so. In order to overcome this, a definite aim or goal must be made first and then every thought and effort directed towards it.

Conclusion: This lady is clearly living too much within herself and is not experiencing fully in the real world outside. As harsh as she may find this, it is essential that she becomes much more of an extrovert and takes an interest in something beyond herself and her limited domestic scene. Fortunately, she has plenty of mental energy in reserve which is not surprising with such a placid nature as hers.

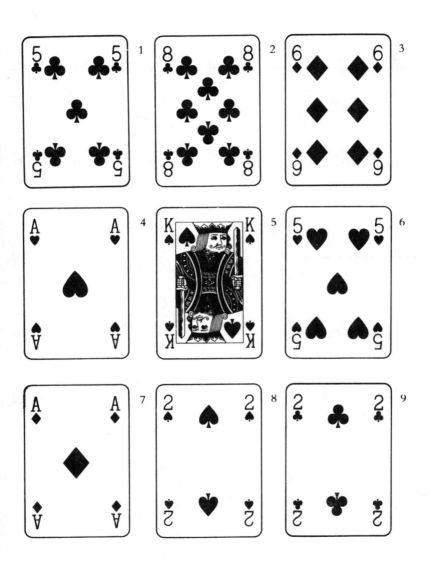

The Magic Square
Psychic Reading

THE MAGIC SQUARE

1	2	3
Individuality	*Duality*	*Stability*
5 of clubs	8 of clubs	6 of diamonds

4	5	6
Tenacity	*Potentiality*	*Opportunity*
Ace of hearts	King of spades	5 of hearts

7	8	9
Spirituality	*Negativity*	*Positivity*
Ace of diamonds	2 of spades	2 of clubs

Psychic Reading
Court Card: King of spades

Combinations and Relationships of the Cards:
Two Aces: Reunion
Two Fives: Uncertainty
Two Twos: Separate ways

Square 1 – Individuality: 5 of Clubs
It is essential for this questioner to know and accept his psychic abilities and his limitations. To over-estimate this is very dangerous yet at the same time to undervalue it inhibits progress. An intuitive middle course should be sought.

Square 2 – Duality: 8 of Clubs
Over-enthusiasm and confidence in personal psychic ability should not be allowed to overshadow the danger from suspect influences which must always be challenged. False prophets who appear as great masters to the unwary could easily divert energy into wrong channels.

Square 3 – Stability: 6 of Diamonds
The questioner should make sure that harmony exists within himself before committing himself into the hands of unseen forces. At all times he must try to keep the balance because this is the only way to ensure psychic stability.

Square 4 – Tenacity: Ace of Hearts

The combination of this card with this square is most fortunate, showing that the questioner has a natural talent for healing and mediumship. This gives him plenty of patience to persevere in situations which so often seem hopeless. It is this quality that has brought him so far along the occult trail and it will continue to do so, so long as he does not over-extract power from this benevolent source.

Square 5 – Potentiality: King of Spades

Here we discover the lone psychic operator. Obviously he is very enthusiastic and has had considerable experience in most of the basic occult arts. His aim is to increase his power by harnessing forces he believes he can control. His potential, however, is not as great as he himself believes it to be and in this lies the danger.

Square 6 – Opportunity: 5 of Hearts

When completely honest with himself the questioner must admit he is lacking in psychic self-confidence sometimes. Although he may not realize it, this prevents him from making the most of his opportunities and eventually will limit him from further expansion of awareness.

Square 7 – Spirituality: Ace of Diamonds

Considerable spiritual awareness has developed from practical psychic experiences and a stage of initiation has now been reached where the questioner is poised ready to move forward into the next phase. Whether or not he will continue with this expansion depends on him and him alone.

Square 8 – Negativity: 2 of Spades

There is a danger of overstepping the mark psychically. By not realizing the power involved in certain rituals, a negative chain reaction could easily start, dragging down not only the questioner but others who are not even associated with his practices.

Square 9 – Positivity: 2 of Clubs

The ability to work both positively and negatively gives considerable power and advantage. This produces very positive psychic results but only the questioner can say whether these are entirely for the good of others or simply for personal increase of power and glory. At this point there is a choice of two paths: one is positively selfless, the other is positively selfish.

Conclusion: This man is very ambitious, psychically. Undoubtedly he is experienced and has made considerable progress since he started on this trail but now a critical stage has been reached where he must choose the left- or right-hand path. Occultism attracts him far more than mediumship although he has a greater affinity with this, as revealed by the ace of hearts. It is on the occult path, however, that he may be tempted to take the wrong steps; and these can never be retraced.

13

THE CELESTIAL CIRCLE

This is a traditional Continental spread, originally using an incomplete pack of 32 cards. When selecting cards from the full pack it gives an excellent indication of events for the coming year, with each card symbolizing one calendar month. The card in the centre reflects the over-all influence for the year as a whole.

Method

Thirteen cards are chosen by the questioner in the true ritualistic way and then handed to the interpreter who turns them over to reveal the first card selected. These are then arranged in the order shown in Diagram 6 (on page 63).

The first card represents the month of the reading so even if it is the last day of the month it must be counted as such. The meanings of each card, on all levels, will reveal the major trends influencing its corresponding month.

If the thirteenth card in the centre is a heart, then a happy year is forecast and if it is a diamond, a successful practical year lies ahead, although probably accompanied by hard work. Should a club occupy this position, money matters and wealth generally will be the centre of attention, but should it be a spade, be ready for a battle.

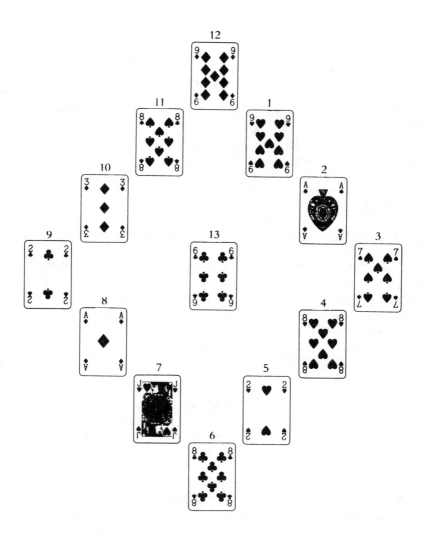

Diagram 6
The Celestial Circle

THE CELESTIAL CIRCLE

                          9 of diamonds
            8 of spades   9 of hearts
            3 of diamonds   Ace of spades
        2 of clubs   6 of clubs   7 of spades
            Ace of diamonds   8 of hearts
                Jack of hearts   2 of hearts
                          8 of clubs

Question: How will my business fare over the coming year?
(Cards selected on 30 September 1980)
Combinations and Relationships of the Cards:
Two Twos: Separate paths
Three Eights: Burdens lessen
Three Nines: Successful enterprise
Two Aces: Reunion

Overall Influence for the Year September 1980 to August 1981

6 of Clubs: Attention will be focussed mainly on money in relation to business matters. Pressure and tension produce considerable worry but if this succeeds in stimulating initiative then it will have been worth the trouble. Experiences will prove invaluable and when they are put to work, will pay off handsomely. By enforcing strict economy measures at the beginning of the year a balance of payment should be reached by the end.

First Month – September: 9 of Hearts
This month has been a happy one closely associated with the family. A holiday atmosphere brought relaxation and a general recharging in readiness for hard work in the year ahead.

Second Month – October: Ace of Spades
A pretty formidable obstacle seems to materialize which obliterates all thoughts of the holiday. Strength and courage will be needed to keep things in perspective but whatever this problem is, it must be overcome eventually. The nature of this set-back is not revealed.

Third Month – November: 7 of Spades

Personal fears and worries will do nothing to solve the problem that developed last month. This breeds negativity so be warned. Relationships suffer and stand the risk of deteriorating through lack of emotional control and any display of bad feelings will be regretted later in the year.

Fourth Month – December: 8 of Hearts

Hopes are high once again but there is an underlying fear of insecurity. All that glistens is not gold, unfortunately, so be prepared. On the more positive side, seeing the situation in its true light dispells all illusion.

Fifth Month – January: 2 of Hearts

An emotional relationship brings a dash of excitement to an otherwise dreary scene. This could be associated with a new romance or it could be that new life revives an old friendship. Socializing plays a bigger part than usual this month.

Sixth Month – February: 8 of Clubs

Financial instability through lack of funds brings worry. Since this card is the gambler's card too, it is worth taking a chance for there is nothing to lose and everything to win.

Seventh Month – March: Jack of Hearts

This could be a most fortuitous month as relaxation and fun bring renewed vigour and hopes for the future. A youthful person livens up the scene and the whole atmosphere is charged with spring.

Eighth Month – April: Ace of Diamonds

The ambition of the year really comes into its own this month. Every effort should be made to attain this goal now or, at the very least, ensure that the road leading towards it is properly laid.

Ninth Month – May: 2 of Clubs

A clash of opinions over money brings progress to a halt. Discussions solve nothing despite joint efforts to reach mutual agreement. Inevitably, a delay is caused but this will be all to the good in the end.

Tenth Month – June: 3 of Diamonds
Having been through a frustrating time, personal determination takes over, ready and keen to achieve that aim. With renewed drive and initiative much will be accomplished this month and although the end object is not quite in the bag, the winning post is now within sight.

Eleventh Month – July: 8 of Spades
Unfortunately, it looks as if an unexpected, last minute setback turns up this month. Suspicion is in the air so no one should be trusted with confidential information nor should they hear personal secrets either. Sit tight and wait for fate to take a hand.

Twelfth Month – August: 9 of Diamonds
Enthusiasm for business is once again on the cards. New ideas, probably resulting from the previous bad experiences during the year will revolutionize the original plans. Expansion all round can be expected and with it will come adventure and travel.

14

THE HEART'S DESIRE

This is not so much a spread as a way to discover, through the cards, whether that special wish will come true. Its origin is said to have been with an amorous member of the eighteenth century French court, so it is strictly for lovers.

Method

A court card is necessary to represent the lover, so this will be one of the heart court cards. It is then shuffled into the pack by the questioner who next cuts this into three separate packs with the left hand, and places them side by side as shown in Diagram 7 (below). The search is now on for the personal court card and the 9 of hearts, the card symbolizing the wish or the heart's desire.

If these two cards are in the same pack, then the heart's desire will indeed be fulfilled. Should they be in the first pack on the left of the questioner then their dream will soon come true. If these two cards are together in the middle pack, then a short delay is to be expected before fulfilment. Should they be in the third pack on the right of the questioner, a considerable delay is seen but all will be well in the end.

When the 9 of hearts is alone in the first pack on the left of the questioner, there is still hope for the heart's desire. If it is alone in the middle pack, the chance is less and if this card is alone in the third pack on the right, then do not bank on things too much.

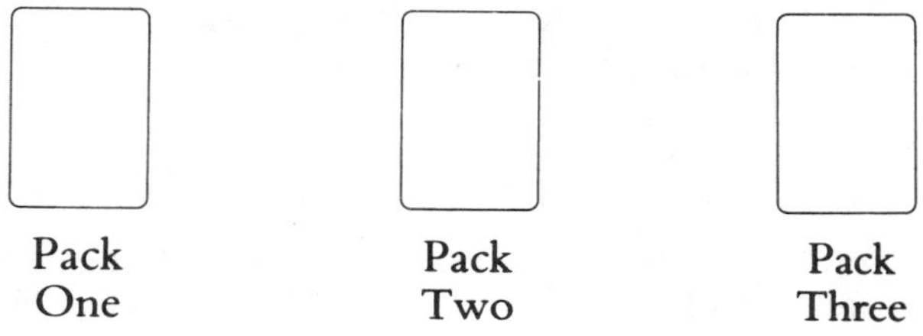

Pack
One

Pack
Two

Pack
Three

Diagram 7
The Heart's Desire

15

THE FOUR SUITS

As well as the traditional associations the four suits have with the greater cosmic plan, whereby they represent the four seasons, the four elements and the four weeks in a lunar month, they also have a strong link with us as individuals. Just as they reflect the principles of above, so too do they reflect the principles of below and it is this aspect of the cards that particularly appeals to our nature. This is because they give us a personal glimpse of what fate and fortune have in store for us.

Generally, we are happy with our heart, diamond and club lot in life but we often wish we did not have to put up with the spades and what they stand for. Unfortunately, these are not only unavoidable but necessary if we are going to learn from our experiences and our mistakes. Even so, a warning given by one of these apparently gloomy cards should never be accepted as a predestined omen of fate. It must be seen as a sign urging us to do something about it. After all, if we do not possess free will, what point is there in us trying to solve even the simplest of our problems! Remember then, that to be forewarned is to be forearmed, so tackle all obstacles positively and determinedly for they must always be far more under our control than we are under theirs!

By looking at life from the standpoint of the four suits, solutions can be seen that are otherwise often missed. Opportunities and successes, true loves and future fortunes shown by the cards help to overcome difficult patches so, in this respect, they are not only prophetic but act as messengers of hope and comfort as well.

Life has four definite aspects, recognized by ancient philosophers and modern psychiatrists and these are symbolized by the four suits. Diamonds represent practical pursuits and material things in life; clubs represent financial matters, riches and wealth; hearts represent emotional feelings and inner responses and spades represent the inevitable problems and obstacles in life.

Everything we think and do arises from one or more of these four standpoints and even a play or film conforms to this four-fold pattern, especially noticed in the characteristic 'surprise ending'. Will it be a diamond-club solution, where the heroine goes for the materialistic jackpot or will she let hearts rule, in spite of an obvious shadow cast by a threatening spade? Real life is just like this.

Diamonds – An Air of Spring
Traditional Aspects
This is the first suit in the pack and symbolizes the spring season and the element of air. It also corresponds with the early part of the day and the morning-time of life. The first breath of spring, with its air of renewal, reminds us of all this for this is the time of birth and rebirth. Buds burst into life and everything in Nature's kingdom starts to grow outwardly. Babies, children and the family tree are associated with this suit.

Practical Aspects
Diamonds are practical, outward-going cards representing material and physical things in life. These include ambitions, aims, work, careers, travel, correspondence and all forms of communication. Logical deductions and clear thinking are expressed, as well as enthusiasm, energy-drives, initiative and high hopes for the future.

Psychological Aspects
From this standpoint, diamonds symbolize the intellect and those who think with their heads. The archetypal intellectual egg-head who often sees no further than the end of his nose when it comes to the real world, extroverts, explorers, high-powered business men and all who follow paths of external pursuit in life are found here. The ancients saw these characters as possessing a choleric nature, one of the four humours recognized by a certain impatience and quick temper.

Psychic Aspects
Psychically, this suit corresponds with positive occultism and all the qualities possessed by those who work in this way. Ability to undertake psychic journeys and astral projection is revealed, along with external forces exerting strong influences. Inspirations materialize as practical ideas.

Clubs – The Heat of Summer

Traditional Aspects

This is the second suit in the pack and symbolizes the summer season and the element of fire. It also represents midday and the peak of life. This is the flowering time and the happy-go-lucky summer of existence, reflecting the heat of the sun, energy and burning desires. Adolescence, with its fires of youth, is associated with this suit.

Practical Aspects

Clubs denote financial situations. Riches and poverty, surprise monetary gifts and sudden expenditures are all within these cards. Personal affinity with money or spendthrift tendencies are shown, as well as indications pointing to the making of potential tycoons, bank managers and accountants, not to mention their opposites, down-and-outs.

Psychological Aspects

From this standpoint, clubs represent determination. Desires to possess money, jewels, property and even other people are indicated. Swinging between moods of hopefulness to states of bloody-mindedness, this type never gives up. Sanguine, the name given to this character by ancient philosophers, sums up their extreme hopefulness.

Psychic Aspect

Psychically, wealth of understanding or poverty of spirit are shown by the cards in this respect. Occult strengths and weaknesses are revealed along with questions of psychic protection. There is a continual quest for enlightenment and psychic fireworks.

Hearts – Refreshing Autumn

Traditional Aspect

This is the third suit in the pack and symbolizes the autumn season and the element of water. It also represents the evening and the maturity of life. This is the harvest time when fruitful rewards are reaped and a mellow, more peaceful stage is reached. Adulthood is associated with hearts and, with its experience, can afford to show compassion for others.

Practical Aspect
Hearts are all about emotions and feelings in relation to the family, friends and lovers. Happiness, fun, relaxation and all social events are symbolized by this suit. Comfort and help given to others increases personal inner strength as surely as does reaping what has been sown. Homely ways and motherly love are predominant.

Psychological Aspect
In this respect hearts represent inner feelings and all who think with their heart. The introvert, the do–gooder, whose excellent intentions sometimes lead other and themselves into trouble and the martyr who makes self-sacrifices are shown. Deep feelings of compassion for all forms of life are expressed too. The ancient philosophers called this character phlegmatic because the person appeared adaptable yet apathetic in relation to external, practical matters.

Psychic Aspect
Psychically, spiritual satisfaction, harmony with the elements and the ability to work well and closely with others is shown. Healing and mediumistic attributes and sensitivity to atmospheres are also revealed. External influences are attracted to strong heart-psychics so warnings concerning protection are revealed.

Spades – *Bleak Midwinter*
Traditional Aspect
This is the last suit in the pack and symbolizes the winter and the element of earth. It also represents darkness and the night-time of life, a time to go to earth, rest and sleep. Benefits gathered from past experiences are mulled over, but cold comfort can lead to depression and sadness. Old age and the human pastime of reflection and regret are associated with this suit.

Practical Aspect
All the hurdles and obstacles in life are represented by this suit. To a certain extent, although these are unpleasant circumstances and events, they serve to straighten out situations in the end. Fair judgment and cold assessment are sometimes very necessary. Health problems and warnings are included

among the hurdles and obstacles.

Psychological Aspect

This aspect of the suit indicates ruthless traits, hang-ups and unwarranted aggression. But hard-headedness often acts as a guise for a much softer inner self who is afraid to emerge, making such people their own worst enemy; they are not as formidable as they seem. Depression and self-pity are revealed. Ancient philosophers saw this character as melancholic, expressing sadness brought on by doubt, lack of self-confidence and bad luck.

Psychic Aspect

From the psychic standpoint this suit represents the dark night of the soul – fears and warnings from the 'great unknown'. Lack of psychic protection and foolhardiness in relation to occult forces invite trouble. Weaknesses and wrong paths are symbolized, as well as downright bad intentions.

16

THE PACK OF CARDS

Each card represents a different aspect, on different levels, of the over-all meaning of the suit to which it belongs. These are its numerical, practical, psychological, psychic, influential and reversed significances which depend on the spread and standpoint from which the cards were selected.

The twelve court cards represent people, as well as certain qualities, whereas the forty numbered cards symbolize situations and circumstances.

The Joker
This card finds its way into a spread in most surprising ways even though it is thought to have been previously removed. The fact that there is a Joker in the pack at all is significant in itself, so he cannot possibly be ignored. So if he does turn up unexpectedly, do not replace him with another card because his presence and message was intended.

Combinations and Relationships
Significant combinations and relationships of certain cards in a spread have collective meanings which give added insight into problems and situations. These are given in the following lists:

Quartets, Triplicities and Pairs
Four Aces	—	Triumph
Three Aces	—	Harmony
Two Aces	—	Reunion
Four Kings	—	Honour and success
Three Kings	—	Good support
Two Kings	—	Good advisers
Four Queens	—	Scandal
Three Queens	—	Gossip
Two Queens	—	Curiosity
Four Jacks	—	Battles
Three Jacks	—	Quarrels
Two Jacks	—	Discussions

Four Tens	–	Change for the better
Three Tens	–	Repayments
Two Tens	–	Change of fortune
Four Nines	–	Unexpected good fortune
Three Nines	–	Successful enterprise
Two Nines	–	Eventual contentment
Four Eights	–	Worries
Three Eights	–	Burdens lessen
Two Eights	–	Inconstancy
Four Sevens	–	Equality
Three Sevens	–	Fulfilment
Two Sevens	–	Mutual love
Four Sixes	–	Unexpected obstacles
Three Sixes	–	Hard work
Two Sixes	–	Contradictions
Four Fives	–	Personal happiness
Three Fives	–	Personal satisfaction
Two Fives	–	Personal uncertainty
Four Fours	–	Equal chance
Three Fours	–	A fair chance
Two Fours	–	Little chance
Four Threes	–	Hope
Three Threes	–	Stability
Two Threes	–	Choice
Four Twos	–	Cross-roads
Three Twos	–	Change in direction
Two Twos	–	Separate ways
The Joker	–	Be not deceived, this is an unknown quantity.

Significant Relationships

The ace of diamonds among several hearts	–	Business and pleasure do not mix
The ace of diamonds among several clubs	–	Matters of business depending on money will come to a head
The ace of spades among several hearts	–	Emotional problems
The ace of spades among several diamonds	–	Obstacles at work or with a career and ambition
The ace of hearts among several clubs	–	Generosity

The ace of hearts among several diamonds	— Love and romance connected with a journey or work
The ace of clubs among several diamonds	— Wealth and an increase of social status
The ace of clubs among several spades	— Financial problems
A number of mixed court cards	— Festivity, hospitality and social gatherings
A court card between two cards of the same number or value	— Someone is supported or hemmed in by their circumstances
A Jack next to a King or Queen	— Protection
The Queen of spades between a King and another Queen	— A break-up of a relationship
The eight and nine of spades together	— A health problem
A Jack among several diamonds	— A messenger will bring important information or news
The nine and ten of diamonds together	— A journey on or over the sea
The nine of hearts and the three of diamonds together	— A stable love-affair

17

DIAMONDS

ACE OF DIAMONDS

Numerical Significance

This is the first and last card in this suit and represents both numbers one and thirteen – unity and rebirth. It signifies a beginning and an end in itself, thus representing a complete project. In this lies an individual's potential and creativity, as expressed through the intellect. Intellectual striving, which should be directed towards one goal at a time, is necessary, even though the seed of success has been sown. This card also contains the power to transform one situation into another.

Practical Significance

In its purest sense this card symbolizes a clear-cut aim for the future. It is a veritable storehouse of energy, sufficient for putting into action all plans relating to practical and material goals. Like the diamond itself, ambitions should be crystallized, then a single-minded approach utilized to achieve these aims as soon as possible.

This card also signifies new business, a new house or new possession, such as a car, furniture or jewellery. An important document or letter which has the power to alter the future is also represented by this card. Such a communication may be sent or received; and those who have taken exams can expect favourable results. It also symbolizes the renewal of hope through intellectual concentration and a more positive attitude, thus encouraging those who have failed in the past to try again. Originality plus drive will bring practical success and material gain.

Psychological Significance

Tremendous drive and positivity produce a forceful character who means to reach his or her goal by hook or by crook. Crystal-clear thinking allows the individual to cut corners and take risks with safety. Unflagging energy and good health aid the attainment of the highest ambitions which others would see as remote castles in the air. A lack of feeling for others may be displayed as this would contribute little to furthering personal ambitions.

Psychic Significance

An occult achievement of some importance is on the cards. This is an initiation which marks a stage of positive psychic development. Inspirational qualities and telepathic gifts crystallize into rewarding experiences which, in turn, produce the confidence necessary for going on to the next phase. One cycle has been successfully completed and the scene is now set for the future.

Influential Significance

This card has a strong, positive influence enabling the individual to direct his or her forces towards the fulfilment of an aim. Businesses, careers and ambitions receive a boost of energy which revives enthusiasm and helps to bring things to a successful conclusion. This influence will override opposition, especially when the aim is for the good of others.

Reversed Significance

Generally this card indicates muddled plans for the future. Good intent remains, but does not receive the stimulation necessary to spark it off. Everything becomes a stumbling-block which overshadows personal potential. A set-back is to be expected.

KING OF DIAMONDS

The King's Significance

This King represents the mature, masculine aspect of this suit.

A combination of experience and action will produce a break-through into new interests. Coming to terms with life has paid off, so the future holds out great promise. On the practical level, stability gives the questioner the confidence to help others as well as to further personal aims. Crowned with success materially, a good basis exists on which to develop other characteristics symbolized by the other three suits.

Practical Significance

Traditionally, this King is the fair-haired, blue-eyed man, muscularly strong and essentially practical. He is a clear thinker who uses his head and prides himself on his successes in business and with women. It may signify a lack of heart and little consideration for others. He is ambitious, reliable, gen-erally honest and his life appears to be an open book. Really, there is more to him than this although it usually goes unnoticed.

   This outward-going personality is naturally disciplined, so a military career would be most fulfilling. As a protector he can be authoritarian yet respected nevertheless. As a business part-ner he will prove loyal and hard-working, but as a marriage partner he needs to be top dog. Romance usually lasts just long enough to convince a woman that he has a heart – then his work takes first place in his life. Whatever else this King may be, he is an excellent business man.

Psychological Significance

Here is an extrovert who thinks almost exclusively with his head. Strength of character gives him figure-head qualities although this does not necessarily mean that his nature is entirely balanced. As his emotions tend to be inhibited he runs the risk of developing into a dogmatic leader. This character-istic becomes more pronounced as the years go by.

Psychic Significance

As a potential magician this King could command and direct the positive forces of Nature for the good of others. Both as a healer and an occultist, his powers will depend on his personal level of understanding and, as he progresses in life and evolves, so will he increase his links with the universe.

Influential Significance

The personal influence from this card is strong and positive. It will persuade others to fall in with your ideas and help things to go to plan although over-enthusiasm and drive may be mistaken for ruthlessness. This influence will help all who are willing to accept hard, unsentimental advice.

Reversed Significance

Strong ambitions develop into devious schemes which eventually undermine stability and confidence. Others lose faith in this King and his plans, with the result that aggression creeps in. Disputes create further problems until the only solution lies in travel or moving to a new home.

QUEEN OF DIAMONDS

The Queen's Significance

This card represents the feminine aspect of the suit. She has a practical and fertile imagination which enables her to compete successfully in a man's world. Independence has been won and she is capable of making important decisions speedily and accurately, often to the annoyance of her contemporaries. A loyal supporter of authority, she is seen as a protective female rather than as a motherly soul. Her ambition is to maintain her well-earned position in life rather than to extend her horizons into unknown territory.

Practical Significance

Traditionally, this Queen has fair hair, blue eyes and a generally pale look. Be not deceived, however, because she is strong, both physically and mentally and knows her own mind. She often thinks she knows other people's too, and this gives her a reputation for being over-authoritative and bossy.

Thinking with her head more than her heart has won her a place in society and brought rewards. As a business woman she succeeds with ease. A career will tend to take precedence over her home and family in the end, although this Queen usually has both these aspects well under control. She is an efficient mother, firm but well-loved. Energy abounds and life always holds out the promise of adventure and change. Organization is second nature to her and demand for her services is therefore great. She is an efficient, positive woman.

Psychological Significance

An unusually positive streak gives this woman an extrovert personality similar to that of a man. Seeing the world as a practical playground, she uses her intelligence to work and play in the best places. Others are jealous of her, but she secretly envies them for their domesticity. As she is so business-like, she is often misjudged as a hard-hearted person.

Psychic Significance

Occult and healing abilities soon develop once this Queen has stepped onto the positive psychic path. Working slowly but surely, she learns to command the positive forces of nature and uses them to help mankind and all other forms of life on this planet.

Influential Significance

Personal influence amounts to self-confidence and self-reliance which, in turn, attracts both friends and hangers-on. These qualities have brought success in the past and will do so again in the future. Others may benefit from this Queen's experience if they take her advice, which is sound and practical, but not always palatable.

Reversed Significance

The hard-headed matriarchal streak is overbearing. When this interferes with other people's liberty, trouble is to be expected. The female who knows it all is not liked and is soon shunned by one and all. In family circles this trait causes breaks which can never be breached; and in business it results in enmity and opposition.

JACK OF DIAMONDS

The Jack's Significance
This card usually represents a boy or youth, in which case he is seen to have a practical approach to life and will show an affinity for business at an early age. He is highly intelligent. If this card symbolizes an adult, however, immaturity is revealed. Ambition exists but remains unfulfilled because hopes are rarely put into action, either through laziness or a lack of real know-how. He is, however, a potential King. So this individual needs to re-orientate himself if he wants to achieve this status.

Practical Significance
Like the King and Queen of this suit, the Jack is also traditionally seen as fair in appearance. His nature is outward-going, sometimes to the extent of becoming overpoweringly extrovert. He is usually a know-all, but is popular nevertheless because of his *joie de vivre* which results from an endless supply of energy. He does not grow old quickly and retains his youthful appearance to the end.

His opinions are well-known, but only a fool would take his advice seriously. At work he makes an excellent boss's man but lives in hopes of one day making the grade himself. Sexually and socially, he is more of a success because in these circles no one need take him too seriously. Sport is really his line for its offers him the opportunities he craves. Alertness and swiftness may even earn him the vice-captaincy of the local cricket team. In the home his intentions are always good and he is full of promises which he cannot, rather than will not, keep. This is an ambitious, youthful male who is the Jack of all trades when it comes to work.

Psychological Significance
Although he is ambitious, this individual is too immature and unpredictable to ever reach his goal. A little success goes to his head and he is not wise enough to follow it through to the next

logical stage. His arrogance is a form of protection, and brooding over the past for too long prevents him from positive forward-planning.

Psychic Significance
As a positive psychic he is often charged with inspiration. However, he should specialize in one of the more mundane occult arts before setting his sights on the higher ranks. He must also be prepared to take orders and obey them, not only for his own safety but for the sake of others, too.

Influential Significance
The personal influence is essentially energetic and youthful even though sound common sense is missing. It is this energy that has helped to keep him going in the absence of real substance. Others may benefit through contact with him by themselves becoming rejuvenated and even inspired. In this sense, this card has a catalystic influence.

Reversed Significance
Stubbornness is his downfall. Unable to believe that he could ever be wrong, his attitude eventually leads to conflict. Untrustworthy and misleading, others may come unstuck through his actions and, in the end, even his charm will let both him and his friends down.

TEN OF DIAMONDS

Numerical Significance
The tenth card of this suit is a sign of completion, indicating that one particular phase in life has ended and another is about to begin. This relates to intellectual and practical aspects: a stage has been reached which is marked by either a change of some sort or an award. It represents a landmark in a career because one goal has been achieved and a step taken on the path to fulfilment. The foundations for future success have been laid.

Practical Significance

A journey which combines business with pleasure will bring a reward. Effort, both physical and mental, is necessary to spark into action a new plan. Past success is not enough, so do not sit and wait too long because a new opportunity is at hand. It is a time for 'off with the old and on with the new' although any loose ends must be firmly tied. Leave no unfinished business before starting on this next new project.

A letter or document will reveal something very important although great care should be exercised in regard to what is committed to paper. A lot of thought is needed to ensure that things start off on the right foot. New buildings or the refurbishing of old ones bring expansion and success, thus laying the foundations for the future.

Life is satisfying on the one hand, but a certain restlessness is felt on the other. This shows it is time to begin something new, or at least to start again on a firmer footing. Plenty of action is symbolized.

Psychological Significance

Extrovert tendencies help increase personal confidence. An active mind needs controlling in order to avoid head-on clashes. Intelligence alone will lead to frustration and a waste of energy.

Psychic Significance

Powerful external forces will be encountered, therefore occult laws must be observed in order to prevent any adverse rebounds. A point of initiation is reached and all who pass this test will gain confidence.

Influential Significance

The influence from this card will produce action although the outcome is not clear at this time. At least it will start things moving. On the practical level, matters will be resolved after an initial period of movement and a certain amount of upheaval. It is time to progress, so new plans should be ready for implementation.

Reversed Significance

A threat of failure will bring hopes and plans crashing to the ground. A lack of direction brings matters to a standstill.

Enthusiasm and drive are replaced by anxiety and fear, thus making the future appear decidedly dark.

NINE OF DIAMONDS

Numerical Significance
The ninth card in this suit is a sign of courage resulting from previous stability. It indicates leadership qualities but warns that such a position should not be allowed to go to one's head and produce a tyrannical boss or over-enthusiastic superior, whose ambitions are achieved at the expense of others. The warning is that the higher one climbs, the further one has to fall. Numerically, this warning is borne out because number nine is the last of the single figures which then return to nought in the unit column.

Practical Significance
New interests are to be expected. These are associated with work, ambitions or practical pastimes and may be connected with a journey or travel. A holiday could prove both educational and relaxing, with long-term practical benefits.

Promotion is offered and new business ventures are assured of success. It is time to start building for the future, so lay the foundations as soon as it is practically possible. Opportunities must be taken when they arise because second chances are not on offer. Energy will be forthcoming as a result of hard work, whether mental or physical, so the necessary drive will not be lacking. Individuality must be preserved although a compromise with co-workers is also required. Too much thinking could overshadow the human aspect of a project, thus preventing the final goal from achieving its blue print perfection.

Ideas begin to expand, even to the extent of building castles in the air because, with the courage of true conviction, these too will one day become realities. Extended horizons are indicated.

Psychological Significance
Single-mindedness brings success although this way of think-

ing needs tempering before it develops into self-righteousness. Stubborn ways prevent full expression.

Psychic Significance
A practical approach to occult matters will bring greater rewards than tackling them from a psychic angle. Positive results can be expected as long as feet are placed firmly on the ground.

Influential Significance
This influence brings confidence and encouragement to the scene. If bold steps have to be taken, these will prove to be easier than anticipated or feared. Practical matters will be resolved best by tackling them in a straightforward way. So be brave and honest in the knowledge that unseen forces are working in your favour.

Reversed Significance
Delays and disagreements hinder the completion of projects and any chance of final success. Lack of courage and self-doubt bring matters pretty well to a standstill. Yet obstinacy prevents a new standpoint from being adopted. Energy is soon dissipated and replaced by a general feeling of disinterest.

EIGHT OF DIAMONDS

Numerical Significance
The eighth card in this suit is a contradiction because it signifies either complete success or utter failure. This is a difficult number: it tends to bring too much of everything and therefore usually amounts to nothing in the end. The ancients saw this as equality and negation, numerically symbolized by the dual proportions two and four. Unfortunately, this makes for indecision all round.

The Practical Significance
Short journeys connected with business and the furthering of aims will be undertaken. Minor aspects associated with other

practical pursuits, including sport, will be to the fore. A visit away from town brings new ideas as well as providing an opportunity to catch up on things.

If things do not go as well as expected, a trip into the country is advised. Getting away, even briefly, gives one the opportunity to see the situation from a fresh point of view.

This card also indicates that too much thought and effort may have been put into a scheme, so take a temporary break. See this stage as a stepping-stone on the way; but ensure that the next move is forwards and not backwards. Much will depend on personal reactions to circumstances, so stand firm. If in doubt, do not make final decisions, but allow time to be the judge. Much will be revealed with patience. There is still plenty of hope and time for a successful outcome, so regard any delays as a necessary evil. Balance and counterbalance are strongly symbolized.

Psychological Significance
Inner conflict produces muddled thinking. Such confusion may apper to be unending because the mind will continually seek outwards for answers. There is little connection between the conscious and unconscious mind at this time.

Psychic Significance
Positive occult forces will accentuate messages from dogmatic religions. These must be recognized and challenged in order to prevent them from influencing the work in hand.

Influential Significance
This influence is likely to bring stalemate and frustration to a situation. It will be difficult to make a move one way or the other: the answer is to wait rather than to be too hasty. Efforts will not meet with immediate results, no matter how much is put into a scheme. However, in retrospect, nothing will have been wasted.

Reverse Significance
Indecision will lead to complications and lost opportunities. Exhaustion results from allowing energy to be wasted in the wrong directions. Loss of drive brings self-recrimination and others, too, are likely to suffer from a wrong move made in haste. It is, however, never too late to start again.

SEVEN OF DIAMONDS

Numerical Significance

The seventh card in this suit signifies completeness in a practical way. It compares with the collectiveness of the seven colours of the rainbow and the seven notes in the musical scale. Representing that aspect which relates to practical hopes for the future, it includes all materialistic possibilities associated with the external world. It is a positive number offering success, provided that the laws of action and reaction are constantly observed.

Practical Significance

This card represents the individual in relation to the outer world. If practical plans for the future have not already been made, then this should be done immediately. It also urges that such plans should be made as simple and concise as possible, then kept firmly in mind as the goal to be achieved.

Representing the personal driving force, this card is closely linked with ideals and ambitions. Artistic talents and everything connected with stage, screen and television are also included. Communicating with others will be easier from now on so, if you have a special message you wish to communicate, get this across as soon as possible. Public speakers and politicians will find this a good time to go into action and the more effort that is put into a project, the greater the benefit is likely to be.

Life will be seen from a fresh angle and renewed hopes stand a good chance of being fulfilled. Energy levels are high, allowing plenty of physical and mental effort to be applied to schemes and activities. A sporting achievement is on the cards too, because the spirit of ambition means to triumph.

Psychological Significance

'Know thyself' through self-discipline is the message here. Yet it is necessary to balance extrovert tendencies with introvert feelings before a true understanding of the self can be accomplished.

Psychic Significance

The spirit will express itself in a very positive way. It may astrally project to far away places and return with gems of wisdom. Dreams will prove most helpful.

Influential Significance

A strong personal influence emanates from this card. Drive, enthusiasm and strength of purpose are ready and waiting to go into action. This will result in the completion of any unfinished business, as well as the initiation of new projects. Material and practical self-reliance is assured, thus generating further self-confidence.

Reversed Significance

Failing to take opportunities will frustrate and annoy unless the general attitude towards life is altered. Wasted talents and an absence of drive and ambition may be due to lack of vitality. A personal stock-taking is necessary: reassess all practical aspects and plans for the future.

SIX OF DIAMONDS

Numerical Significance

The sixth card in this suit symbolizes possibilities and ambitions which are often difficult to achieve. Practical plans and material possessions tend to lack real substance even though a lot of hard work has been put into them. This number carries a warning message that one can fall to the ground if caught between two stools, so complete one project before starting on the next one.

Practical Significance

Documents in relation to property, business, work, careers and aims are symbolized by this card. A dispute is likely unless extra care is taken when signing important papers or agreements, so read the small print carefully. On a personal level, refrain from committing to paper anything that could not be repeated in public. Information leaks could cause trouble, as could indiscreet statements made in personal letters.

Much is going on behind the scenes although this may not be apparent at this time. A situation could, therefore, appear to be a paradox. Plans to travel may be upset at the last minute although they will right themselves at the eleventh hour. At work, disagreements due to unforeseen circumstances result in delays although no permanent damage is caused; in the home, differences of opinions arise over practical issues. Relying on the intellect too much produces a one-sided view of a situation. If logic is abandoned, a sudden flash of inspiration should occur to throw light on everything.

Psychological Significance
Material worries weigh heavily and cause tension. Difficulties in accepting the true situation aggravate negative tendencies. So beware of disagreements and bad tempers all round.

Psychic Significance
Beware of instability within a group of positive occultists. This could be due to the absence of negative-receptive psychics who would redress the balance.

Influential Significance
This influence is conveyed mainly through the written word. The pen is mightier than the sword, especially in business matters, so watch out for misconstructions, misleading statements and verbal barbs. Action is necessary to restore stability, therefore this influence should be utilized for this purpose.

Reversed Significance
If allowed to continue, undercover actions will disrupt plans. A lost document or letter will delay the completion of a project and hopes for an early settlement will begin to fade. Be prepared for last minute set-backs owing to the unreliability of others.

FIVE OF DIAMONDS

Numerical Significance
The fifth card in this suit symbolizes mankind, full of practical hopes and potential for the future. From the germ of an idea, it is possible for a far-reaching plan, which has the power to alter one life or many, to develop. This card offers fulfilment, but it is up to the individual to accept or reject the challenge.

Practical Significance
This card holds great promise for the future, providing that opportunities are taken when they arise. There is plenty of originality, but this requires drive to accomplish anything lasting and worth-while. Difficulties may be encountered initially but, once started, the road to success lies ahead.

A move from present property to new or different accommodation is indicated. A journey is in the offing too, providing a change of scenery; this could be a holiday or a business trip. Education and matters associated with the increase of knowledge will come under review, and changes will need to be made in order to get the best results.

Promotions and improvements are there for the asking but, again, it is up to the individual to take the opportunities offered. This is a testing time, but those who are ready and willing to face the challenges will reap the benefits of their hard labours for a long time to come. Personal opportunities which should not be missed are symbolized.

Psychological Significance
Stability of the outward-going aspect of the personality will help achieve extrovert ambitions and goals. This aspect has developed independently from the opposite, introvertive side, so attention should be paid to the heart as well as the head from now on.

Psychic Significance
The urge to work alone should not be encouraged. Positive

psychism within the group will bring safer and surer individual progress as well as results.

Influential Significance
This influence highlights practical failings as well as abilities. It gives an opportunity for one to discover weaknesses and strengths and it is therefore worth-while taking the time to learn in which direction your real talents lie. New plans should be laid on the foundations of past experiences. This will make the most of the positive aspects because these hold out the promise of eventual success.

Reversed Significance
Frustration, due to lack of success, does little to put matters right. If ever perseverance was needed, it is now; so try, try, try again. A journey could cause extra inconvenience, but any action is better than none, so make the best of things and go with the stream, not against it.

FOUR OF DIAMONDS

Numerical Significance
The fourth card in this suit is not an easy card to accept. As it represents the square of two, it adds complications to any situation which already offers two alternatives. If determination and logic are applied, the result will be a firm victory and progress; but if dithering and indecision are allowed to take over, then all semblance of a set plan will disintegrate.

Practical Significance
Whichever way you look at this card, difficult decisions arise. Opposition to even the most carefully prepared plans are inevitable; even last minute alternatives are likely to appear as if from nowhere. These difficult choices are likely to arise in matters relating to jobs, business, new houses, material possessions and holidays: everything, in fact, concerned with the practical side of life. Even letter-writing is likely to pose problems.

Too much consideration of a problem or situation is just as bad as too little, however, because both add up to a null and void. In intellectual circles, contradictions produce anger, mainly because there is more than a grain of truth in the opposing points of view. This disrupts stable beliefs, with the result that insecurity creeps into the situation. This is not the right time to make decisions. It may even be a question of the time of the year because the four seasons have a very powerful effect on all mundane matters. What might be easily accomplished in the heat of the summer is an impossibility in deep midwinter.

Psychological Significance
Instability is expressed in extrovertive ways and other people notice this. Hang-ups associated with work produce exaggerated characteristics which scare away others, even friends.

Psychic Significance
Occult forces do battle to unbalance the situation. Constant protection and challenging is necessary. When contacting and manipulating these powerful forces, they must not only be guarded against but recognized for what they are and what they can do. To reverse the balance of power, use their mirror image.

Influential Significance
This influence pulls in many directions at once. Loyalties to colleagues, on the one hand, are at loggerheads with what is practically best, on the other. Deals tend to cool off as a result. Communications with others are difficult because of crossed lines. So, when in doubt during this period, do not commit your comments to paper or air them verbally.

Reversed Significance
Fragmented plans and impossible ideas waste time and energy so it would be better to scrap everything and start again. Only by concentrating on one aspect at a time will any real progress be made. There is a lack of co-ordination between hopes and the implementation of them: a stalemate situation exists.

THREE OF DIAMONDS

Numerical Significance

The third card in this suit has a built-in stability which can provide help for practical aims and ambitions. It is a good sign, indicating that now is the time to take a step forward because your plans are based on firm foundation. Creativity should blossom from this point and as this card signifies a source of knowledge, further original ideas can be expected. Confidence in practical ability encourages the expansion and development on all fronts relating to business, hobbies, pleasure and leisure.

Practical Significance

Plans for the future are on a firm footing, but determination to see these through to a successful conclusion will be necessary. If this is lacking, even the best laid schemes can founder, so focus your attention on the final objective and keep this in view all the time.

Energy is available for physical and mental work, so utilize this without delay. Original ideas are waiting to be recognized and, when they are, they should be applied to any old projects which require new stimulus. Academic theses, symbolized by the Cambridge tripos exams, are represented by this card. Thus, intellectual work will suddenly become easier as the barrier to knowledge is pushed back. This is a good time to think about exams and tests because any results from these should be excellent.

Ingenuity, originality and determination make ideal partners in the practical and intellectual fields of life, so it is not surprising that this card symbolizes a blend of past, present and future hopes.

Psychological Significance

Positivity produces a very determined and outwardly stable person. Too much determination could develop into selfishness, however. So, if you do not wish to appear to be on an ego trip, match this determination with thought for others.

Psychic Significance
Harmonious relationships with psychic co-workers and positive occult forces will bring great spiritual rewards. Help and healing directed now will give good results.

Influential Significance
Should lack of enthusiasm slow down practical, material or intellectual progress, then this influence will introduce determination onto the scene. As a result, positivity and drive return, bringing the end object within grasp. Hard work is still necessary, but with this incentive it will seem much easier to achieve positive results. A form of isolation could be experienced as the result of utilizing this determination, but a 'go-it-alone' course is likely to prove far more rewarding than one which is dependent on the whim of others: the prize does not have to be shared, for one thing!

Reversed Significance
Owing to laziness or lack of drive, a distinct difficulty will be encountered in the achievement of a hope, ambition or project. A plan is desperately needed to escape from the present circumstances which are static and frustrating. Physical efforts are liable to be wasted as things now stand, so try to take stock of the situation.

TWO OF DIAMONDS

Numerical Significance
The second card in this suit is a paradox. Two practical aspects have to be considered and united into a whole, if at all possible. Two heads are better than one — except when they disagree with each other. All or nothing situations develop and the introduction of an alternative is bound to throw something out of balance temporarily.

Practical Significance

This card offers partnerships and delicately balanced relationships between two people linked through business, practical working arrangements or the domestic side of marriage. Both should contribute to the whole by using their individual experiences to bring about a productive joint situation. When the aim is the same, harmony exists; but if one party loses sight of this objective, disharmony will result.

It is difficult to keep a balance all the time because duality tends to make final decisions very difficult; and knowing there is a choice only makes things worse. Communication between partners could lead to trouble too, because meanings are not conveyed properly, so extra care must be taken when expressing a point.

If progress with plans slows down, take one step at a time. Good ideas are lacking because parallel lines can never meet – seek out the balanced way. Great tact will be necessary in order to prevent a permanent rift, yet if the right cards are played, agreement and unification will eventually result.

Psychological Significance

Split intentions divide attention on the practical front. Thoughts tend to run in parallel lines which never converge. Energy is wasted, so tiredness is to be expected.

Psychic Significance

Difficulties with two positive aspects confuse occultists. It is easy to go down the wrong psychic track so be careful to challenge all forces in use.

Influential Significance

This influence brings duality which will not always help a current situation. Since this has the effect of introducing a choice or alternative solution it is only later that its true value will be seen and appreciated. Indecision is the worst aspect but, on the other hand, it is important to ensure that the other side of the coin is not forgotten either. The reward from this lies in the future, not the present.

Reversed Significance

Ambitions will be overshadowed by obstacles and practical difficulties. Opposition to a plan makes matters seem impossible and any amount of hard work will have little or no effect. An all or nothing situation has developed, with the result that there is the possibility of falling between two stools.

18

CLUBS

ACE OF CLUBS

Numerical Significance

This is the first and last card in the suit. It combines the numbers one and thirteen which, together, form a pool of wealth. This gives stability and security to individuals as well as firing them with the enthusiasm necessary to search for that proverbial pot of gold at the end of the rainbow. This card is a power in itself and needs careful handling but, if used with discretion and understanding, it attracts all the good things in life. On one level it brings materialistic prizes and, on another, the wealthy reward of wisdom.

Practical Significance

Good fortune lies in this card. Wealth is on the horizon and is well within the questioner's grasp. Speculation has paid off handsomely, bringing material comforts and plenty of worldly goods. There is a warning though; remember the saying: 'Easy come, easy go' because this is a possibility. Permanence is not a special feature of this card, so watch interests carefully.

The way in which such financial wealth is used is most important. If rewarded as one of the talents it will bring help and happiness to many people. So, casting bread on the waters of life can result in rich rewards for everyone. Those who have used personal ability to attain high standards in life will be rewarded with national or even international fame. Industrious folk will reach their goal through inventiveness and devotion, whilst others may well inherit money or titled status.

At one end of the scale this card can signify a big pools win, a legacy or a generous gift; whilst at the other, it represents recognition as a star performer, politician or actor.

Psychological Significance
A strong desire to possess objects of material value over-shadows the simple things in life. You should allow those underlying characteristics which lie nearer to your heart to express themselves.

Psychic Significance
A special psychic gift will come to light. If this is used accord-ing to occult law, a great wealth of understanding will add to an ever–deepening pool of wisdom.

Influential Significance
The influence from this card instantly helps flagging financial resources. It brings respite from money worries and allows the individual time to reorganize his or her affairs. Although this may not solve the problem, it will certainly give an oppor-tunity to recuperate funds. Speculation and a new approach to wealth will develop, so use this influence to attain a particular goal or standard.

Reversed Significance
Dependence on money for security and pleasures in life will soon reveal the lack of substance such a pursuit brings. Dis-satisfaction, linked to an inability to alter course, produces frustration and poverty of pocket and outlook.

KING OF CLUBS

The King's Significance
This King is the experienced man, crowned with financial success. A stockpile of worldy goods allows time in later life to pursue wealth on a higher plane. Self-confidence arises mainly from material assets, but opportunities will arise later which should put this on a more intuitive footing. Imagination is not

lacking, but if this is directed one way only, it will lead to limitations. A collector of most things – from valuable antiques to a load of old rubbish – this King is seen to be a very single-minded person, with an eye for making a quick profit.

Practical Significance

Traditionally, this is one of the dark, rich-complexioned kings, full of life, sexual vitality and good ideas. Many seek his advice, mainly because he appears to have done so well for himself. Although he is completely trustworthy as far as his intentions go, he may lack sufficient experience to be considered an expert.

Tycoons and financiers are represented by this card and, very often, it is their single-mindedness that has brought them to the peak of their success rather than careful, intelligent planning. Ruthlessness possesses such individuals when they are on this road to success because they know that if they weaken or are deflected off course, they stand to lose.

When this king is the big fish in a little pond, everyone knows it. Modesty is not among his attributes and being in demand is one of his greatest pleasures. Acting as the kingpin suits him and he guards his territory jealously; those who take liberties are castigated, but those who come with cap in hand are more than welcome. In this attitude, shades of insecurity can be seen and this trait is found in even the richest of financial wizards.

Psychological Significance

This king possesses the good quality of perseverence. This attribute should be used with discretion, however, or it might be mistaken for over-forcefulness. He has a rich pool of experience from which to draw but, again, care has to be taken or he could appear boastful.

Psychic Significance

Even though he is an experienced psychic, he still seeks proof that other dimensions really exist. Until he can accept these instinctively and intuitively he will remain at his present stage of initiation.

Influential Significance

This gives control over finances and wealth generally, so

influential help with any monetary problems can be expected. This may come from an experienced person qualified in banking or from a changed situation. Loans, if needed, arise from reliable sources and, although expensive, will restore that lost security. A fortunate gift of money or a useful present will brighten life temporarily but, for permanence, this card's influence should be utilized to put personal affairs in order.

Reversed Significance

Miserliness produces a narrow mind that shuts out the true meaning of life. Greed, deception and covetous ways eventually lead to loneliness. The individual's inability to accept changes results in personal limitations and, unless care is exercised, leads to a hermit's life. Fear of losing what has been hoarded encourages false suspicions to develop, so that family as well as friends stay away from the door.

QUEEN OF CLUBS

The Queen's Significance

This Queen is the feminine aspect of the suit. She is an efficient, successful woman who is used to plenty of money and knows what it can buy. Material luxuries often become a necessity so that when times are hard and these are lacking, she becomes unsociable and bad tempered. As a business women she has her own interests at heart, rather than those of clients or customers and can, therefore, be regarded as somewhat self-centred. A rich husband is often her source of wealth but, when needs be, she has a good head for making money.

Practical Significance

Traditionally, this queen represents a dark-haired, richly complexioned woman. Active and generous, she enjoys charitable work and organizing others into action. She often acts the lady bountiful, expecting compliments and admiration for her efforts. Wealth, her prop and support, will occasionally be used to promote others, but they are expected to show her endless gratitude in return.

These characteristics show up more and more with increasing years yet, should she find herself alone, she is well able to look after herself and become the bread-winner. Her place, she feels, is in the home but not around the kitchen sink; so any opportunity to go out is seized upon immediately. Lavish in most respects, she is always well and fashionably dressed. Most men admire her cool, sophisticated appearance, but few realize just how expensive she can be until it is too late!

Vitality gives this queen an attraction which makes her the envy of other women, who tend to be jealous of her. This is probably why deep friendships are virtually non-existent. In sports she finds the perfect setting to prove and show herself off; usually, she excels in these and wins many prizes.

Psychological Significance
This woman is an independent thinker, a characteristic which has its benefits although loneliness may develop later through lack of proper communication with others. Her need to possess material objects shows that she looks outwards for security instead of inwards, where personal reserves wait to be recognized and tapped.

Psychic Significance
Occult work is carried out positively and negatively. This brings a wealth of experience but also highlights personal psychic strengths and weakness.

Influential Significance
Personal self-confidence will receive a powerful boost from this positive influence. A temporary self-centredness may develop, but this is just what is required at this time. The effects are generally uplifting, so you can expect an increase in wealth which acts as a safeguard against impending trouble as well as allowing you the time to think and replan for the future.

Reversed Significance
This represents a mean, bad tempered and suspicious woman who cannot keep a friend for long. Always greedy for more and wanting to keep up with the Jones's, she becomes inquisitive and prying, with a result that more doors close than will ever be opened. She is her own worst enemy.

JACK OF CLUBS

The Jack's Significance

When representing a boy or youth this card shows that there is a strong desire to reach the heights and become head boy, captain of the cricket team or the organizer of interests other than the three Rs. Although not an academic, he is a budding tycoon because he has the ability to accumulate wealth and fortune.

If representing an adult, this card represents one who is stuck on the treadmill of life. The result is that this individual never hits the jackpot which was once well within his range.

Practical Significance

Full of vitality, he enjoys taking on responsibility at an early age. Able to save money, he soon learns the advantages that a nest-egg provides; therefore his talents turn automatically towards hoarding more and more. He will always make a determined effort to keep a bargain, although his personal aim or ambition will always be first and foremost in his mind. It is often said that he has an old head on young shoulders yet to put implicit trust in him would be most unwise.

Experience is what is needed and this, combined with the exuberance of youth, holds out great possibilities. To achieve kingly status he must beware of the trap which would keep him at his present knavely level for the rest of his life. How successful he is in this aim will depend on how adventurous he is when opportunities arise.

A degree of risk is involved in making the grade, so chances must be taken if true aims and ambitions are ever to be achieved. This Jack is the only one who can afford to take such chances and get away with it.

Psychological Significance

This character finds difficulty in keeping to one thing at a time. Hopefulness makes up for this defect and carries him through to a limited success. He has the ability to see ahead but does not always rely on his own judgment. Other people let him down yet he does not seem to learn his lesson.

Psychic Significance
Seeking answers to profound occult problems will prevent steady psychic progress. Don't expect too much too soon or a sharp encounter with a restraining occult force will bring a quick realization of your folly.

Influential Significance
This influence will help boost resources and thus restore faith in oneself. It may manifest as a loyal supporter or as a financial improvement. A racy atmosphere will help to relax any previous tension, so be bold and take a chance on a project, idea or hope. Back hunches to the full because this opportunity may not be repeated for some time.

Reversed Significance
Over-enthusiastic drive produces a dicey character who is regarded as potentially dangerous. The higher he climbs, the further he has to fall and, unfortunately, a fall is on the cards through his own stupidity.

TEN OF CLUBS

Numerical Significance
The tenth card in this suit indicates the completion of one phase and the beginning of the next. The perfection of this number, the first of the multiple numbers, can be compared to the wheel of fate and fortune. Wealth – on all levels – has been accumulated in the last cycle and the future already rests on a secure footing. The phase ahead offers opportunities which, if taken, will provide further increases.

Practical Significance
A welcome sum of money is on the horizon, possibly from an unexpected source. This may materialize in the form of an inheritance, gift or a big gambling win. Security results, thus

generating feelings of confidence and anticipation. But be prepared for surprise complications which could temporarily delay the actual arrival of this money.

Much revolves around investments and assets – from the largest fortunes down to post–office savings – so do not let these lie idle for too long. Like the talents in the parable, these will repay you best by being made to work.

This is a good time to spend money on investments for the future, so now is the time to give serious consideration to ways of doing this. Do not sit back and take it easy at this stage or rely too much on past glories. Drive and action is essential to keep the wheel of fate and fortune turning.

Psychological Significance
Hopes will be recharged with energy through personal effort. Fears and doubts are left behind as a new cycle in life begins. Forget the past and look ahead to better times.

Psychic Significance
A gift from the gods helps psychic progress. Philosophically, this represents the harvesting of a previous sowing: good actions have been followed by good reactions. A new level of awareness is achieved.

Influential Significance
This is a strong, positive, monetary influence which will bring security and confidence to a particular situation. Expect financial matters to stabilize and then steadily improve. Much strength and comfort is given by this material asset and although it is meant to be used, do so only after very careful consideration. Try to insure against future expenditure by acting now. An opportunity to do this will arise shortly.

Reversed Significance
It is virtually impossible to alter present spendthrift habits and, as a result, the last of personal savings ebb and unpaid bills mount up. Without money to act as a form of security, incentive is missing and this keeps the doors of opportunity closed.

NINE OF CLUBS

Numerical Significance

The ninth card in this suit is very fortuitous because it attracts further stability in the form of wealth, in every sense of the word. A peak in financial affairs will be reached shortly and this will bring respite from worries. Also, a milestone has been reached, which puts things on a much firmer footing all round. However, this does not mean that it is a foregone conclusion that the future is going to be rich, without any effort being made. In order to maintain this stability, efforts will be needed and now is the time to make plans for this.

Practical Significance

Wealth is definitely on the cards. Bank balances will soon look much healthier, possibly due to inheritances, gifts or money from property. Any money owing will also be repaid. One-man businesses will benefit financially, offering the opportunity for further expansion. Material comforts and a lessening of pressure will follow.

Money connected with marriage and close friendships is closely associated with this card. Over-all richness is indicated, but partnerships will need constant attention in order to continue to function as profitable propositions. Marriage settlements following divorce or separation are to the fore and any uncertainty concerning money will end soon. This is the right time to complete outstanding financial arrangements, even if the sum involved is small. Once this is done, freedom from worry follows – and this is a gift in itself.

A prosperous marriage is also indicated although this does not necessarily signify pounds in the bank. A wealth of happiness and mutual understanding accumulates, too. Count your blessings now and they will become a good investment for the future.

Psychological Significance

Confidence reaches a peak. Negativity vanishes, albeit tem-

porarily, so make the most of this opportunity. Good relationships in the home and at work produce a relaxed and happy
atmosphere, resulting in peace of mind.

Psychic Significance
Positive and negative psychism blend and harmonize, thus
opening up even more doors on the occult scene. A wealth of
new experiences are offered and confidence in one's own
ability increases.

Influential Significance
Decisions will be influenced by money. As a deciding factor,
finances rather than emotions should be used as the yardstick.
Joint savings will produce unexpectedly good results. This
influence has a stabilizing effect too, and although things may
appear to slow down it is only temporary. This will give you a
valuable opportunity to catch up before moving on to the next
phase.

Reversed Significance
Present financial stability cannot last much longer. Expenses
will increase enormously and quickly outweigh income, so
expect high personal inflation. Steps should be taken now to
prevent a landslide into poverty.

EIGHT OF CLUBS

Numerical Significance
The eighth card in this suit strongly suggests a balance of
payments. Riches, on all levels, are difficult to assess at this
stage and can be compared with a half full or half empty glass
of water: it all depends on the individual standpoint. A rest
may be safely taken at this time before starting on the next
phase. There is a danger of covering the same ground again by
repeating the past, but there should be no turning or looking
back, only forward.

Practical Significance

This is the gambler's lucky card. The desire for money and wealth is strong although, at this point, there does not appear to be a watertight plan to bring this about. The solution offered is to take a risk because this is the chance card. Bypass the usual channels and jump in at the deep end, knowing that you stand a very good chance of winning.

On the basic level, play your hunches because inspired guesses about which dog or horse will come in first can be relied upon. Gambling with property and investments, where financial rewards are high, are good bets too. Those not given to risking their shirts should at least be adventurous when investing, buying or selling.

This is a 'nothing ventured nothing gained' situation and unless a positive move is made now, progress will be circular, so beware of arriving back where you started. A bottle-neck has been reached, indicating that the past must be completely settled before turning to the future.

Psychological Significance

Difficulties in understanding personal motives cause worry. Too much self-analysis will only lead to confusion and further complications however, so accept yourself and others for what they are.

Psychic Significance

Powerful influences could easily divert good intentions into the wrong channel. Beware of false values and false prophets who unbalance normally stable psychic atmospheres.

Influential Significance

This influence brings out latent gambling instincts and the desire or necessity for more money will develop. This trend will force some form of action to be taken. Opportunities will arise and these should not be ignored or missed because they can save a lot of time and effort by allowing you to take a short cut to the jackpot.

Reversed Significance

By repeating past mistakes more financial losses will be incurred. A negative vicious circle traps the unwary, with the result that it will become impossible to escape even further losses.

SEVEN OF CLUBS

Numerical Significance

The seventh card in this suit signifies personal success in life and offers security and insurance against the future. Carefully planned efforts have paid off and produced a nest-egg of considerable size. On other levels, too, wealth has accumulated and this may be used profitably in many different ways.

Practical Significance

This card represents the natural ability to make money and attain materialistic goals. Involvement with financial matters at this time is likely and if the right cards are played, success is ensured. Ambitions and plans concerned with making money, or even a modest living, need to be constantly watched. Past experience shows that this will pay off, so don't let go of the reins now or the initiative will be lost as a result.

Since wealth is comparative, individual situations must be seen in relation to personal circumstances and standpoints: £1 seems a lot to some people but nothing to others. Special care must be taken when dealing with other people's money in order to safeguard personal reputations. Honest intentions are not enough: indicate on paper exactly where the money was spent.

Financial success is definitely on the cards, but due more to personal effort than to good luck. However, ensure that your values do not alter and do not make money into a god.

Psychological Significance

Freedom of self-expression should be encouraged now, using the wealth of past experiences to do so. A mature outlook has developed and should be of great help in solving life's problems.

Psychic Significance

Individual psychic development takes a big step forward. After an exciting phase, doors will open on new dimensions.

The value of controlled astral travel will result in an important initiation.

Influential Significance
Personal financial matters will improve considerably with the help of this influence. Businesses benefit too and the domestic front will remain in funds despite heavy outlays. New ideas on how to budget and increase income will develop and this will, in turn, bring the security which has often been lacking in the past.

Reversed Significance
Total disregard for simple accounting brings personal financial troubles. Heavy debts will eventually lead to serious circumstances that could involve others who are in no way to blame. The days of borrowing are past.

SIX OF CLUBS

Numerical Significance
The sixth card in this suit offers a choice of ways in which to make money and obtain wealth but is not a solution in itself. Much hard work and plodding effort are necessary to bring things together, which will be essential before a move forward can be made with any degree of confidence. Pressure and tension are inevitable, yet these will produce the driving force necessary to start to pull things into shape.

Practical Significance
Help will come from a most unexpected source. This could signify a fortunate turn of events or may indicate that a reliable friend will offer profitable advice. Another possibility is that a loan of hard cash could materialize. So, one way or another, some form of enrichment can be confidently expected.

Income and expenditure will just about remain on an even keel. There is nothing to spare, however, and since there is nothing to cover an emergency either, strict economy measures must be implemented at once. This is not a permanent situation but any action taken now will have good repercussions in the future. Careful planning is all-important, so don't be tempted into rash spending or investing in dicey holdings.

Reliable advice is worth seeking before parting with cash, and such help will be found easily although it may not come from a conventional source. Use instinct along with intellect to forge ahead: using both together will allow a more balanced assessment to be made. Everything must ultimately be paid for in one way or another, so do not forget to make provisions for this.

Psychological Significance
Doubts and fears should be seen in perspective or they will upset balanced judgment. Keep negativity under control by replacing dependence on others by self-reliance.

Psychic Significance
Expect occult influences to manifest in strange ways. Personal coincidences will initiate a new train of thought which will lead to new psychic pastures. Psychic development progresses slowly but surely.

Influential Significance
A helpful influence from out of the blue saves the day. Projects and plans relating to business and family matters which depend on money will benefit greatly. Last minute rescue measures will turn up trumps with the result that disappointment will be avoided and good friends will prove themselves to be as good as their word. Faith is restored all round.

Reversed Significance
There is a tendency to underestimate and overspend. An 'easy come, easy go' attitude may work for a while but, once the scales have been allowed to tip too far in the wrong direction, poverty is on the cards. Such conditions are self-imposed although this does nothing to stop the negative, downhill slide.

FIVE OF CLUBS

Numerical Significance

The fifth card in this suit denotes hopes for a better future. With drive and iniative, plus plenty of inspired guesses, it is possible to work up from nothing to a richly endowed position in life. This could result through an accumulation of material assets or, alternatively, through a wealth of experience. The end objective is quite clear although the road to this success has yet to be fully laid. Taking a new track altogether could provide a solution.

Practical Significance

Money associated with marriage and partnerships is indicated. This may take the form of sharing gifts and inheritances or the taking of rewards from joint business efforts. If equality is absent, a financial arrangement may leave one partner hard up, however, so changes might be necessary. Even though this might mean starting from virtually nothing, it will be worth all the hard work in the end.

Seen as a challenge, an opportunity will present itself which will bring better returns than a previous investment. There is nothing to stop progress once a firm plan is made and, should money troubles develop, they will soon vanish because, once started on that positive road leading towards the end objective, cash will begin to materialize.

Long-term monetary plans, including pension schemes and insurance policies, should be considered now. With an eye on the future – looking especially in the direction of old age – it pays to ensure that the nest will always remain well feathered.

Psychological Significance

Difficulties in dealing with others could become a worry. Weakness of character can lead to mental oppression, so it is important to recognize this tendency before it is too late. To keep the peace is one thing, but to be overpowered is another.

Psychic Significance

Positive psychic protection is necessary when controlling occult forces which are stronger than is realized. Harmony within the group will help to develop this, but if harmony is lacking, unwanted influences will creep into the situation and cause havoc.

Influential Significance

This influence will have long-term effects on wealth generally. At least this will settle things one way or the other and reveal the true financial state, down to the last penny. This can be regarded as a definite starting point, so look ahead and make those much needed plans for the future. This card holds out great promise that things will go well, provided that personal dedication is applied positively.

Reversed Significance

Lack of initiative in the past continues into the future and there is little hope of any opportunity, however good, being taken now. Financially broke, friends are thin on the ground. Devious means of recouping losses will not provide a solution, however, so such thoughts should be squashed.

FOUR OF CLUBS

Numerical Significance

The fourth card in this suit indicates a struggle to keep things on an even keel. Resources could be drained in several directions at once, leaving little in reserve. However, if a halt is called now, a firm basis is left, upon which a secure, four-square future could be built. If arrangements involve partners, special care must be taken to maintain the necessary harmony and balance or all could be lost completely.

Practical Significance

There is a strong warning in this card concerning the loss of a valuable article. Extra precautions should be taken to ensure that material possessions such as keys, jewellery, purses or gloves as well as cash, cars or furniture are not stolen or lost. The call on financial reserves could be a lot heavier than anticipated and limitations imposed as a result. The solution lies in keeping well within the bounds of solvency.

A loss of faith in oneself leads to lack of self-confidence and to lack of trust in others who have, in the past, been most reliable. This can cause insecurity, so keep the question of balance in mind when trying to regain equilibrium. Equal but opposing forces will either negate and destroy each other or harmonize into a positive force which can help to stabilize the situation.

Psychological Significance
Inhibitions seek outlets and, in so doing, may appear as extreme behaviour. Mental highs and lows produce mood swings, but this is only a temporary stage and will pass. Try to steer a middle course, especially when in the presence of others.

Psychic Significance
There is a risk that too much psychic work will drain off too much energy. This will not help anyone, so take a rest from occult encounters in order to keep at least one foot on the ground.

Influential Significance
Demands from several directions at once produce an influence that draws heavily upon resources. So, expect savings to dwindle and, on a physical level, be prepared for energy to drain away. Since it is difficult to do much about things at present, it is best to sit tight, relax and wait for a change of atmosphere.

Reversed Significance
Extreme difficulties will be encountered regarding money matters. Distrust of everyone and everything brings negotiations to a halt and produces an infuriating stalement. Snap decisions will invariably be wrong, so do nothing rather than make more mistakes.

THREE OF CLUBS

Numerical Significance
The third card in this suit offers stability in respect of resources. Acting as a reservoir from which to draw, businesses
will recover and thrive, and the launching of new projects will
prove remarkably easy. Enthusiasm fires ambitions into
action and things will grow from this point into profitable
reality. Those who have experienced failure in the past should
try again, for the time is now right to make another attempt.

Practical Significance
Financial stability gives the materialistic self-assurance which
has been lacking until now. Progress in all directions is on the
cards, although opportunities still need to be recognized and
grasped before they will pay off. There will be good co-opera-
tion between partners and this, plus firm financial backing,
signifies that plans, schemes and proposals stand every chance
of success.

A stage has been reached where new and profitable ideas
will emerge on many levels. In a mundane respect, financial
benefits from an expanding business can be expected. From a
personal standpoint, valuable past experiences will be put into
action to form a source of wealth from which to draw when in
trouble and in need of strength of purpose.

Individual potential invested in business, artistic pursuits or
on the domestic front now will express itself in very rewarding
ways. Excellent foundations exist on which to build for the
future, and now is the time to do this with every confidence.
There is more than a grain of truth in the saying 'third time
lucky', so prove this right by acting on intuition backed up by
experience.

Psychological Significance
Reserves are high, bringing mental stability and confidence in
oneself. Unification of ideas will blend into a new creative
stream of thought, leading to future fulfilment.

Psychic Significance

The occult 'law of three requests' is encountered. When challenging entities and forces, use this law in order to be absolutely certain of their true identity.

Influential Significance

This is a stabilizing influence which gives confidence and introduces security into schemes and projects. Money matters will begin to look a lot healthier soon and will continue to improve for some time. A prosperous atmosphere shines on the domestic front, so extravagances are excusable just now.

Reversed Significance

Self-reproach for wasted opportunities leads to aggression and anger. As hopes fade, they are replaced with despair but, since no effort is made to really alter, this must be expected.

TWO OF CLUBS

Numerical Significance

The second card in this suit indicates a duality which is likely to produce head–on clashes and opposition associated with wealth and its distribution. Discussions with partners or financial advisers appear to offer no solution, yet, at the same time, efforts must be made because nothing ventured means nothing gained. Eventually, the balance will be restored, but keep an eye on both sides of the fence until this happens.

Practical Significance

A change of circumstances brings uncertainty but this is inevitable. In practical terms, money matters prove worrying although real fears for the future are quite unfounded. The joining of forces is one answer to the problem but, since this is not yet possible, it is better to go it alone.

Although joint efforts may appear to halve responsibilities and liabilities, they could, at the same time, double mental strain through such an arrangement. One aspect has, therefore, to be weighed against the other. On the whole, any pressure to pool resources should be resisted in the knowledge that a lone effort will more than double rewards.

The reckless spending of money or energy will not be recouped easily, so this is not the time for action generally. Projects launched now have only a fifty-fifty chance of success; therefore, it is better to wait for a sign that leaves no doubt whatsoever that the time is right and the door wide open.

Psychological Significance
The conscious and unconscious minds form a link which increases awareness and understanding of oneself and others. Care must be exercised, however, in order to maintain a good balance between the emotions and the intellect. Further development of the character will grow naturally from this duality as long as a careful balance is maintained.

Psychic Significance
Working as both a positive and negative psychic will increase the individual's powers tremendously and result in a greater degree of responsibility. A good, balanced philosophy of selflessness and compassion is very necessary therefore because the welfare and safety of others is at stake.

Influential Significance
Although this is an opposing influence it often does a lot more good than harm in the end because it lessens the urge to spend unwisely on non-essentials. The twin nature of this card inhibits positive decisions, yet, again, this acts as a brake just at the right time and thus protects resources. Do not throw caution to the winds however, but stand with both feet firmly on the ground in readiness for the next phase.

Reversed Significance
Opposition destroys every vestige of hope and kills enthusiasm. Vindictive partners inhibit self-expression and make life thoroughly miserable. Double the price has to be paid for innocent mistakes.

19

HEARTS

ACE OF HEARTS

Numerical Significance

This is the first and last card in the suit: a combination which produces fulfilment and wisdom. Nourishment to feed and sustain all heartfelt desires stems from this and happiness is initiated too, which affects all emotional situations. New friendships and reunions are activated, offering lasting friendship and love in the future. As a source of energy, this manifests on many levels, beginning with sexual and physical attractions and going on to compassionate feelings for humanity and all living creatures as a whole.

Practical Significance

Everything the heart desires is in this card. A happy family, true friends, passionate lovers and continued peace of mind are all definite possibilities. Heartfelt hopes and wishes stand a very good chance of being realized because fate and fortune shine benignly on the happiness scene at this time.

A surge of benevolent energy from this source of plenty rejuvenates and heals tired bodies and minds. Having received this, kindly feelings and thoughts for others are generated which, in turn, reward the individual with a satisfying, inner harmony.

Socially, opportunities arise which offer the chance of meeting many new friends and those in search of a lover will find themselves in the right place at the right time. Romantic settings materialize in the most unexpected places and relationships blossom speedily in this atmosphere. Sex and excitement soon enter the scene and these are followed, more often than not, by long-standing arrangements. Fertility is also symbolized by this card, so the beginnings of a new family circle could follow suit and the whole cycle of life begin once again.

Psychological Significance
Strong emotions need to be controlled because the heart definitely rules the head at this time. Judgment could well be very unbalanced from this singular standpoint although a good balance should develop eventually, once it is realized that a one-sided outlook exists.

Psychic Significance
A pool of compassion and understanding is ready and waiting to be tapped by those who wish to do so. Healing energy arises from this source and may be utilized for self-healing or directed towards others who need it. This force pours oil on troubled waters and protects the innocent.

Influential Significance
This is a strong, compassionate influence which can be used in any situation that lacks love and understanding. It will calm down the irate, bring balance to an over-materialistic situation and, by introducing humour into a worrying monetary problem, remove fears completely. Purely in its own right, this card has the power to introduce emotional happiness and inner satisfaction.

Reversed Significance
A barren situation is to be expected. Lack of understanding, absence of feeling for others and a general bleakness dispels all hope of emotional happiness. A big disappointment results in loneliness – with a broken heart hiding beneath a shattered exterior.

KING OF HEARTS

The King's Significance

This King is the great lover of the pack. He expresses himself with deep feelings coloured by the dictates from his heart. His ambition is to collect plenty of admirers and notch up sexual conquests but, with the increasing years, he turns more towards philosophical concepts. In many ways, he is a self-centred person and cannot see himself as he really is. He sincerely believes his heart is in the right place and that this is enough.

Practical Significance

Traditionally, this King is a fair-haired, blue-eyed man who is very emotional and thinks mainly with his heart. Above all, he is a great lover. This makes him a warm-hearted person who is friendly, kind, generous, well liked and popular. He is the home-loving type and therefore puts this side of life before his career and materialistic ambitions. As a father he plays for hours with the children.

Since he is an incurable romantic, he attracts the opposite sex and takes them in, completely. Flattery and compliments pour from him and he has the gift of bestowing himself on one woman at a time, creating the impression that she is the only person in the world so far as he is concerned. Inwardly though, he is really a loner who exists in a secret place surrounded by his own thoughts. Others rarely know him although they often think they do.

His artistic nature can be channelled into various directions and, in the home, often manifests as a pretty garden and, at work, as a tidy desk. This neatness makes up for his apparent lack of originality although this trait is not lacking when it comes to pursuits nearer to his loving heart.

Psychological Significance

Heartfelt emotions nearly always hold sway over reason and logic. He has a great need to love and be loved, compassionately as well as sexually. There is a danger, however, that this individual will become withdrawn as he grows older.

Psychic Significance
Strong receptive qualities show good mediumistic ability which, when partnered by positive psychic communications, will extend well into the 'great unknown'. This King may also represent masculine discarnate beings such as departed fathers, uncles or grandfathers.

Influential Significance
This is the loving influence, whether from a lover, parent or good friend. It has the power to persuade and charm the birds off the trees, if necessary. Sometimes glib words accompany it and are accepted as pearls of wisdom, but only time will tell if these are true or false. Advice flows freely from the heart although, since this is based on emotions not on sound, practical experience, it cannot really be taken too seriously.

Reversed Significance
A tendency towards selfish sexual gratification does nothing to fulfil the desires in the long run. This attitude may attract a wide circle of off-beat acquaintances, yet such company will only end up by being despised thoroughly.

QUEEN OF HEARTS

The Queen's Significance
When young, this character represents the lover, and the blushing bride. As she grows older, she becomes the comfortable little woman in the home whose limited outlook extends little further than the end of the garden. She tends to develop interests which focus solely around the kitchen sink, and a bit of gossip. Ambitions are at a minimum beyond this point, yet contentment seems to grow rather than diminish with time.

Practical Significance
This Queen is generally regarded as a fair-haired person, yet

this exterior, like the superficial image of all the court cards, is unreliable. When a girl, her hopes dwell on an early marriage, a home of her own and a family.

Potentially a ready-made mother, a good friend to the neighbours and a thoroughly domesticated person, she asks for no more than peace and quiet in the home. Romantic notions make her queen of the kitchen where she takes pride in cooking, cleaning and everything within the scope of the domestic scene. Once married, however, her standpoint changes. She drops the glamour – which once lured every male in sight – for a stouter, almost dowdy image of the mistress of the house.

Artistic talents grow with middle-aged spread and what emerges usually surprises everyone: pretty paintings and romantic story-writing were invented for the typical Queen of Hearts.

Emotions are slowly conquered over the years and self-assurance grows from inner self-satisfaction rather than from intellectual confidence.

Psychological Significance

Seeing life from an emotional point of view gives a very one-sided picture. This leads to over-sensitivity and, eventually, to self-pity. Introversion should be counteracted by more outside interests in order to restore the balance as soon as possible.

Psychic Significance

This Queen is a natural medium. It is important that she learns to control this gift properly, however, before uninvited influences intrude and take over. Good protection is essential, therefore. This card may also represent feminine discarnate beings, such as departed mothers, aunts or grandmothers.

Influential Significance

This influence offers good motherly advice. Compassion and a reliable shoulder to cry on help to release tension, particularly as confidences will be respected. A friendly atmosphere restores harmony both inside and outside the home and, generally, happiness reigns.

Reversed Significance

A self-centred outlook limits a fertile imagination and this eventually frustrates and demoralizes a normally placid nature. Friends become few and far between and interests diminish. Day dreams replace practical plans and further obstacles prevent emotional happiness. Dreariness overshadows the domestic scene.

JACK OF HEARTS

The Jack's Significance

As a boy or young man this knave is full of fun. If he matures emotionally he will become the King of Hearts, yet he will always retain that boyish look throughout his life. Potentially a kind person, he seems to miss out when it comes to hand outs and experiences difficulties in being taken seriously. This causes frustration. A general aura of immaturity – a characteristic which, once recognized, is never forgotten – makes him the symbolic Peter Pan.

Practical Significance

He is, like the King and Queen of this suit, traditionally fair. Easy-going all his life, he enjoys sport more for the sociability it offers than for the exercise. Although a competitive spirit is lacking, a sporting attitude to life is not – so he is very popular, especially with the ladies. At work, promotion seems to pass him by, but since happiness and an easy-going life are his chief aims, this does not bother him unduly.

When in love he can be hurt easily and shows it, too. His habit of wearing his heart on his sleeve does not help in this respect and he is prone to make unfortunate relationships anyway. When married, he is often thought to be his wife's son because he is virtually ageless.

Even when he draws his retirement pension this individual still has a boy's face. But this youthful exterior does nothing to alter the funny old character who has developed over the years, inside. Kindness must be acknowledged, however, for this is basic to his naive nature.

Psychological Significance

This Jack does not take himself seriously and should, there-fore, not expect others to do so either. He is amiable, poetic and a day-dreamer, yet becomes bored very quickly. Practical interests should be developed or depression will creep in all too soon.

Psychic Significance

Intuitive and meditative, he has the makings of a good initiate. However, this enthusiasm quickly fades when it is discovered he has to start at the bottom in order to reach the top. Be warned: psychic dabbling could develop if persistence is lacking.

Influential Significance

Without a doubt this influence brings a dash of renewed vigour, especially to a flagging sex life. Such physical rejuven-ation surprises everyone and a much more relaxed atmosphere replaces tension, so life will be happier and more fulfilling than of late. Friends rally round and social gatherings provide opportunities for meeting new faces and visiting exciting places.

Reversed Significance

As the unhappy lover of the pack, he makes himself more miserable than is necessary by wallowing in self-pity. This – and pride – prevent him from snapping out of it and, eventu-ally, he takes on the role of the dejected lover, permanently.

TEN OF HEARTS

Numerical Significance

The tenth card in this suit shows that another round of the emotional side of life has been completed. The culmination of this cycle manifests as inner peace and confidence. A new phase begins soon, built upon the foundations of the past, and plans for the future concerning the family, love-affairs and all happy events should be made without delay. Changes are inevitable, but these will be welcomed.

Practical Significance

A very special and pleasant surprise brings happiness and joy. Rewards from past efforts bring unexpected gifts and a happy event. This could be news of a baby, an invitation to a wedding, a family gathering, a party or a reunion with a long-lost friend or lover.

There is a feeling of anticipation in the air. This acts as a protection against negative acts by producing a buffer effect. Progress for the family as a whole is to be expected and inner satisfaction brings long hopes for happiness to the individual. Romantic encounters are on the cards, so lovers can look forward to an especially exciting time when they will be able to devote more time to each other than they thought possible.

Although business and pleasure do not usually mix this is one of the few occasions when one will help the other. Social contacts and entertaining lead to expansion of material benefits, so do not hesitate to invite the boss to dinner. If you are the boss, then give employees a treat and you will be repaid by loyalty in return. This is a time when compassion, friendship and generosity can well be afforded.

Psychological Significance

The prospect of destiny suddenly becomes very important. Inner motives can be examined by deep thinking, yet there is no time for this now because action is needed, not more inaction.

Psychic Significance

A successful cycle, concerned mainly with negative receptivity, mediumship and clairvoyance, has been completed. A change in psychic direction will follow, and this will introduce the more positive side of occultism onto the scene.

Influential Significance

This is a strong protective influence which guards against emotional agony and trauma. Personality clashes will bring no lasting damage and quarrels and misunderstandings will soon be patched up. There is an element of surprise in the air and the introduction of unexpected events will result in much happiness, making life lighter and more relaxing.

Reversed Significance

Romantic opportunities are missed, with a result that self-recrimination follows. Negative emotions create tension which builds up to bursting point. This will clear the air, but also warns that the same unrewarding cycle will begin all over again unless the situation is recognized for what it is and changes made.

NINE OF HEARTS

Numerical Significance

The ninth card in this suit is considered to be the most fortunate in the pack and is known as the 'wish' or 'heart's desire' card. Therefore, all who are concerned with serious love-affairs and matters close to the heart can expect complete fulfilment. As the square of three, this number has stability as its main characteristic. Courage to make romantic approaches and confidence to see things through to the end will suddenly develop as a result of this.

Practical Significance

A high romantic note is reached where the world seems a beautiful place. Since everyone loves a lover, everything in the proverbial garden is lovely too. Those who harbour a secret wish can expect this to come true . . . with just a little effort. Positive steps must be taken to ensure that the desired result is achieved because it takes two to make a bargain.

Apart from these good romantic indications, family affairs will prosper too. An abundance of goodwill flows from within and this affects all who come into contact with it. Life seems really rosy and troubles are at a minimum.

An opportunity will soon be offered to fulfil the heart's desire yet this could be missed unless personal effort is added to it. To a great degree, future happiness depends on the outcome of this opportunity, so be prepared to grasp it with both hands.

Psychological Significance

Solitude becomes a most satisfying experience. Experiencing a complete inner life strengthens purpose and causes illumination to shine into the lesser known, dark corners of the mind. Complete peace of mind brings great happiness.

Psychic Significance

Harmonious relationships between psychics produce excellent results for the good of all living creatures. Healing acts are particularly effective at this time and hopes in this direction will be more than realized.

Influential Significance

This influence is truly romantic. Hidden desires will be ignited and an imminent meeting with a lover is on the cards. Life in general is going to become happier and more exciting as a result of this prevailing atmosphere. Now is the time to make a wish, knowing that it stands a good chance of coming true.

Reversed Significance

The over-romantic atmosphere encourages lovers to make fools of themselves, so beware. Over-enthusiastic behaviour will result in your intentions being misunderstood and the object of the heart's desire will be thoroughly put off. Too much sentimentality, on the other hand, could ruin a plan just as easily as could an overtly sexy approach.

EIGHT OF HEARTS

Numerical Significance

The eighth card in this suit is a paradox because it signifies possibilities which result either in perfect harmony or in bitter disappointment. There are no half measures, so expect all or nothing situations to develop. The difficulty arises when final decisions have to be made; yet, if this can be accomplished, immediate peace of mind is achieved. If friendships are not as satisfying as they should be, now is the time to make a break and start again.

Practical Significance

Happiness is offered, at a price. Superficially, everything appears to be going well but, inwardly, a feeling of emotional uncertainty exists. Apply positivity to the situation and ignore negative signs as much as possible because these are less important than they seem. Forget the past, if possible.

If proffered gifts are accepted as tokens of true affections and not as appeasement presents, any temporary disagreements with family, friends or lovers will soon be forgotten. Social events, romantic moments and sentimental journeys will bring joy to the heart but, again, try to ignore all aspects which threaten to undermine present happiness.

Sensitivity is now at an all-time high, so be careful not to jump to the wrong conclusions, especially where affections are concerned. Feelings of guilt are likely and this could lead to inner conflict. Hasty action will be regretted later, so turn a blind eye to certain things.

Psychological Significance

A split mind exists which takes time to put together again. Deep feelings are at loggerheads and the only way to unite these is to turn your attention to outer, practical aspects where a real solution may be found.

Psychic Significance

A choice between two psychic paths has to be made. This must be decided by the individual, who should in no way be influenced by the group. Forces of equal intensity will make this a difficult decision, however.

Influential Significance

The influence from this card throws new light onto old situations associated with matters of the heart. There are two sides to every question and these will be shown up very clearly. Even so, do not expect to reach conclusions easily because patience will be needed in order to maintain harmony.

Reversed Significance

Prejudice will prevent an alternative course of action from being seen, let alone taken. One-sided views, if allowed to persist, will bring eventual destruction of emotional relationships and leave a void which will be very difficult to fill.

Obstacles in the path of love and opposition to sentimental journeys will be virtually impossible to avoid.

SEVEN OF HEARTS

Numerical Significance

The seventh card in this suit is complete within itself and signifies great personal potential for happiness in the future. Everything the heart desires is contained within this card and, provided the game of life is played according to the rules, wishes and hopes will surely be granted. Self-satisfaction is justifiable for this has been earned as a result of philosophical reactions to life's problems.

Practical Significance

This card represents individual desires for personal happiness and reflects the emotional aspect of the self: that which is known only to the individual concerned. Secrets of the heart suddenly become very important because now is the time to do something about them. Stability has developed from past experience, bringing a quiet confidence with its own attractiveness and mystique. So, if this is combined with positive drive, all those romantic dreams can come true. However, if indecision is allowed to creep in, they will, unfortunately, fade all too quickly.

An opportunity will occur shortly which will offer the chance to express artistic talents. This could have far-reaching effects and lead to considerable success or even fame. So now is the time to take stock of dreams and hopes and begin working towards achieving them. New avenues should be explored, too, especially those which bring a diversion from everyday problems.

Psychological Significance

An excess of emotional energy must be allowed to express itself freely or there is a danger of it rebounding as nervous tension. This represents the libido, the basic driving force which, according to Freud, needs a regular sexual outlet.

Psychic Significance

A mystical experience will bring enlightenment and under-standing. The symbolism of this signifies a key to the store of unconscious wisdom and, depending on the school of occult-ism followed, will appear in relation to the Holy Grail, The Tree of Life or the Tao.

Influential Significance

This is a strong personal influence, capable of steering emotional and heartfelt circumstances towards desired con-clusions. Compassion and understanding has a calming effect on disturbed individuals and on difficult situations. Lovers may confidently expect a good response from those they desire most and should ensure, therefore, Cupid's dart aims for the right heart.

Reversed Significance

Failure to make the most of a romantic situation will be bitterly regretted. Hopes for a special meeting with someone will be frustrated through lack of initiative and courage. A disappointment in love is on the cards, entirely due to personal neglect and not through lack of opportunity.

SIX OF HEARTS

Numerical Significance

The sixth card in this suit brings the heart's desire nearer, but at a price. Two sets of circumstances are at loggerheads, yet, for peace of mind, they must eventually merge somehow because a compromise is inevitable. One may hope for the best of both worlds but, since this card does not symbolize actual fulfil-ment but only a step on the way, no immediate conclusion should be expected.

Practical Significance

This card symbolizes some form of self-sacrifice, either self-imposed or the result of unfortunate circumstances. Accept-ance is the only answer at this stage, although this does not mean that everything has to remain unchanged. One may be willing to pay a high price for something the heart desires above all else, yet it is foolhardy to take this to the extreme of enforced martyrdom.

To be at the beck and call of the family or having to take a back seat in someone's affections amounts, in principle, to the same thing. A one-sided love-affair or an eternal triangle situation is a notorious breeding ground for willing self-sacrifice.

This card warns that the heart should not be allowed to dictate unconditionally because self-destruction moves in all too quickly, replacing happiness with pain. If this is regarded as a necessary experience then much can be learned but, when looking back on things, nothing should ever be regretted.

Psychological Significance
There is no inner peace at present. Independence is desired but fears of standing alone prevent progress towards this. At least this is an aim in the right direction, so it should become the goal for the future.

Psychic Significance
Psychic abilities should be used in the service of others. This is a testing-time, so expect clairvoyance and all the occult arts to be thoroughly scrutinized and challenged by superiors.

Influential Significance
This is a personal influence which could eventually make a rod for your own back. It allows others to take advantage and exploit your loyalty, yet, at the same time, it encourages the pure sacrificial act which is a gift to those who are genuinely in need of help.

Reversed Significance
Masochistic tendencies attract other people's burdens as well as your own, which will all weigh heavily upon your back. Emotional energy drains away and physical hard work is on the cards too. If this situation is allowed to continue, inner rebellion will cause untold trouble and mental turmoil. Self-help is the first line of defence, therefore.

FIVE OF HEARTS

Numerical Significance
The fifth card in this suit symbolizes the need to communicate with someone and fulfil that friendship. Sexual relationships, especially on the romantic level, need careful handling because emotions could destroy practical stability and ruin everything. Happiness is encouraged although this could be missed through the implementation of a short-sighted policy. So, play for time: think of tomorrow as well as of today.

Practical Significance
'Still waters run deep' is the message of this card. It signifies a strong urge to escape from true feelings, due to divided loyalties or a guilt complex. The heart and soul have been put into an amorous pursuit at the expense of reason, so caution is needed before all bridges are burnt.

This is a severely testing time when heart-searching questions need honest answers. Actions taken now will have far-reaching effects and, since these arise from the emotions, considerable restraint is needed. Sexual desires must be strictly controlled or they could be misunderstood. Equally, other strong emotions which also need curbing are those likely to erupt as passionately religious beliefs or nationalistic outbursts.

At this time the truth is difficult to recognize and face. Sometimes it lies beneath excuses which lead to negativity and inaction; at others it manifests in positivity and over-reaction, bordering on extreme fanaticism.

Psychological Significance
Guilt emerges as self-pity one moment and as aggression against others the next. Frustration due to lack of emotional outlets causes a build-up of mental energy which should be released physically, in the form of sex or sport, or expressed mentally through philosophical concepts.

Psychic Significance

A lack of confidence in one's psychic ability brings development to a halt. Communication between the conscious and unconscious mind has been neglected, but the way will open up again once this fact has been recognized.

Influential Significance

This influence encourages one to escape from real issues. It is the 'bury-the-head-in-the-sand' card but, unfortunately, such behaviour will not send troubles packing. A brave heart is needed above all else. Strength seems to gather from nowhere once the world has been faced because others will then make moves which will help to improve the situation tremendously. The first move must, however, come from within the individual.

Reversed Significance

Turning a blind eye to personal affairs presents others with the opportunity to take unfair advantage. Laziness plus cowardice heaps more troubles on the old ones, so there is an urgent need for a change of direction. Heaven–sent opportunities still arise but are consistently ignored.

FOUR OF HEARTS

Numerical Significance

The fourth card in this suit tugs at the emotional heart-strings. There is a fear of toppling too far one way so that life appears to be rather like walking a tightrope just now. Beware of jumping out of the frying pan into the fire, yet, at the same time, do not simply sit there: something must be done but the question is, what and when?

Practical Significance

Emotional independence is represented by this card. This has developed not so much from happiness but more through painful experiences which tore at the strings themselves. Having reached this singular stage, fear of showing one's true feelings exist and emotions now act as a barrier which keep romantic encounters at bay as a result. Members of the opposite sex are viewed with distinct mistrust and lack of confidence in them and oneself has formed a negative alliance.

In family circles disharmony rules. Arguments and disagreements may well give cause for concern yet, if this situation is faced fairly and squarely, much of the heat can be removed and things will then be able to simmer down generally.

Swinging from the heights to the depths emotionally makes for unstable situations and relationships, so this is not the time to make bold decisions which could very well be regretted later. It would be better to do nothing than to spoil the future but, if action is unavoidable, try to take steps which are not guided solely by the heart's wishes. Remember, the head should have its say too.

Psychological Significance

Swinging emotions produce manic-depressive moods. If external circumstances are to blame, concentrate on keeping a middle of the road course. If it is inner feelings which colour and trigger matters off, learn to recognize the two extremes of temperament and blend them mentally.

Psychic Significance

The importance of the four-fold nature of matter is indicated with this card. This suit represents water which, in turn, symbolizes compassion, understanding and feelings for others. The further development of these qualities is needed before a four-square psychic footing can be achieved, however.

Influential Significance

This has an unsettling influence on the emotions. Its origin is found in past bitter experience which is best forgotten if future happiness is ever to be won. Sometimes it provides protection against complicated love affairs; at others it opens the door onto one-sided relationships which drag on to become forlorn romantic hopes. Sit tight and wait for the winds of change to blow.

Reversed Significance

Unfair deals in love bring inner misery. Nothing will ever happen to change things, therefore it is advisable to try to forget the past, accept the present and plan for a better future. Familiarity breeds contempt, so do not make this mistake on top of all the others.

THREE OF HEARTS

Numerical Significance

The third card in this suit shows emotional stability with considerable control over personal feelings. A quiet confidence attracts others of like natures and a new-found strength of character gives added encouragement to pursue the object of the heart's desire. Fertility, birth and rebirth are symbolized by this card, too, on all levels.

Practical Significance

Romantic happiness can confidently be anticipated. A new-found emotional stability increases attractiveness, so lovers should find life particularly fulfilling. Friends and family appear more amenable than usual and everything goes smoothly and swimmingly.

Those who are madly in love can expect a reward for their devotions and one way in which this expresses itself is in an increase from two to three. A new baby could be the one to make up this number . . . so be prepared.

Fertility of imagination is also ready to produce its brain child which, like its physical symbolic counterpart, is full of potential and hope for the future. It is as if a long period of training is over and, having completed the course of sowing, the reaping is about to begin. What follows is the harvest: a prize of which to be truly proud. Abundance of emotional happiness should be stored and treasured for a rainy day.

Psychological Significance

Emotional stability has been won through personal effort. This is a superior mental state which bestows strength of purpose to aims and ambitions of a practical nature. Expect progress with underlying plans.

Psychic Significance
The still, inner voice of intuition should always be heeded and respected. Original psychic techniques and unique remedies for healing arise from this source.

Influential Significance
This influence restores any lack of self-confidence. If there is a yearning for a particular partner then this new-found inner stability will attract him or her in the right direction. A surplus of mental energy creates a much more stable atmosphere, so life should grow happier and easier all round.

Reversed Significance
Emotional effort is wasted in the wrong direction. Relationships prove most unsatisfactory owing to poor judgment of character. Lovers and friends seem unreliable, but the truth is that the fault lies much nearer home. Do not take sides in three-cornered arguments where no one can win.

TWO OF HEARTS

Numerical Significance
The second card in this suit holds the key to harmonious relationships where two hearts beat as one. Whether two can live as cheaply as one is another matter however, so the diamonds and clubs must be consulted in this respect. Individually, a good relationship has developed between the inner and outer selves, resulting in a much more expansive outlook on life.

Practical Significance
Marriage and all romantic partnerships are represented by this card. Chance meetings and renewed acquaintances will blossom into deep and happy friendships, some ending in marriage, others not. All sexual relationships – from the first

kiss to the finality of making love – are also symbolized by the two hearts on this one card. Plenty of give and take, partners in themselves, are needed to maintain this delicate balance, but this can be done quite successfully when there is a joint aim.

Apart from lovers, relationships between friends, neighbours, workmates and family flourish, so there should be plenty of fairness and equality all round. This is a good time to iron out any differences and long-standing disagreements. Such troubles may well come to a head, so be ready to deal with them with a compassionate heart.

The merging of ideas will more than double the rewards and you should not let pride keep progress from the door any longer than needs be. This is the time to unite in theory, if not in practice.

Psychological Significance
A natural sense of justice and fair play paves the way for a greater understanding of action and reaction, sowing and reaping, Yin and Yang. These are the basic principles of psychology as well as those of the universe as a whole and produce inner peace as well as an outer atmosphere of harmony.

Psychic Significance
Telepathy between well balanced psychic partners leads to further occult initiations. Working in pairs will increase awareness safely and surely as long as a unified aim exists.

Influential Significance
This is a dual influence affecting hearts and emotions. The opportunity for shared romance and joint happiness is offered, probably arising from social activities or holidays. A generally peaceful atmosphere reigns, allowing time to rest and catch up on the more neglected aspects of family life. Shared experiences bring joy and laughter.

Reversed Significance
Disharmony between lovers, friends and family is on the cards. Emotional relationships are very unstable and disagreement all round makes life intolerable. Revealing personal feelings to others will lead to further misunderstandings and only make matters worse.

20

SPADES

ACE OF SPADES

Numerical Significance

This is the first and last card in this suit and combines numbers one and thirteen into a source of trouble. This is seen as a necessary evil because it brings into the open that which festers beneath the surface. The force behind this has the power to leave no stone unturned and in so doing reveals some pretty unpleasant surprises.

Practical Significance

An enormous hurdle or challenge in life lies in this card. It brings to a close one phase and starts off the next so this is why it is often seen as the death card. Life is staged throughout in phases and many of these end on climatic notes; the symbolic death of a love-affair is one such example. Death, therefore, is by no means the only finality we have to face, as this card signifies.

Underlying problems relativing to health, business, money matters, love-affairs, ambitions, careers and hopes for the future will be affected and are bound to come to a head soon. Action will be forced upon those who ignore the warning signs so be prepared. A sense of justice rules too, which often appears ruthless for the natural law of action and reaction does not take feelings into account. On a practical level, law suits are possible concerning tussles over rights and possessions but a philosophical approach, where everything is fair in love and war, helps soften such blows. So face up to challenge and, where necessary, accept these events as inevitable stumbling blocks along life's highway.

Psychological Significance
A mental hang-up prevents real enjoyment, satisfaction and happiness from life. This is the iceberg of the mind where only the tip shows and the rest lies dangerously submerged beneath the surface of the unconscious. The first step towards thawing out this condition is to accept its existence and know its extent.

Psychic Significance
Beware of unseen dangers. Occult attacks through foolhardiness could bring fear and trepidation to even the most experienced psychic workers. Keep up protection and challenge every entity and force thoroughly. The effects from this cause disharmony within the group and loss of confidence in the individual.

Influential Significance
This influence adds fuel to the fire that needs just a spark to set off an inferno. Once this happens it must be fought with might and main. It has the power to disrupt situations and turn placid people into aggressive lunatics who collectively start riots and even wars.

Reversed Significance
If things could get worse then they will. Forsaken by friends and life generally, injustices appear on all fronts producing a trap from which escape seems impossible. Enormous personal effort is needed to alter the present downward trend where problems are forming into immovable obstacles.

KING OF SPADES

The King's Significance
This King is the archetypal judge attracted to authoritarian positions in life. He is often found in local government, politics and the professions, especially law. Dogmatic and severely critical, he is quick to see faults in others but fails to notice his own. With a ruthless logic devoid of all compassion his intellect rules stubbornly over his instinct and intuition. It is

better to have him as a friend than a foe.

Practical Significance

Energy surrounds this dominant and positive character. He uses this ruthlessly and unstintingly to further his own ends and once he is on the ladder of success he means to stay there until he reaches the top. He is most professional in everything he does and nothing short of perfection, often at the expense of others, will do. This leaves no room for the slightest criticism from others but, to be fair, he does his job very well indeed.

When at work he crosses swords with everyone who stands in his way. Since popularity does not go with either his job or his character he remains a loner. There are two types of women who are attracted to him; the masochist who enjoys being the underdog and the more than equal female who means to be top dog. She controls him from the start, much to everyone's delight and surprise.

Beneath the armour of over–confidence and self–opionionated superiority there actually lies a streak of insecurity. To cover this up he over–reacts and, in so doing, reveals his weakness.

Psychological Significance

There is a danger of a dynamic personality being ruined in later years through greed. In pursuit of power, patriarchal tendencies could become tyrannical but if these are tempered with wisdom, true leadership qualities emerge. Cruel traits exist which must be curbed.

Psychic Significance

Striving to invoke the four elements, this potential wizard or warlock seeks power and not wisdom. By contacting forces which he later finds to be beyond his control, he eventually falls under their spell although would never admit this.

Influential Significance

This influence produces single-mindedness and a ruthless approach to life. It gives power to enforce decisions and law and order which, in certain circumstances, is essential. There is always the danger of overstepping the mark and becoming too dictatorial, so the utmost discretion is needed.

Reversed Significance

A lonely destiny lies ahead for this cold, calculating character. Pursuits of power have led him along a path strewn with obstacles and trouble which eventually build up into insurmountable barriers. Chaos and disorder rule completely.

QUEEN OF SPADES

The Queen's Significance

This Queen is ambitious and ruthless in pursuit of power. She rules the roost wherever and whenever she can and makes others well aware of their subordinate pecking order. A stickler for discipline she rarely takes other people's feelings into account when she lays down the law. Thinking exclusively with her head enables her to achieve feats more sensitive women would never desire, let alone strive for.

Practical Significance

There is no need for an enemy with a friend like this woman. Friends to her are there to do her bidding and nothing else, but she loses most of these after their first encounter with her selfish temperament. Committee work attracts her and it is not long before she takes command, including the chair. Since she is far from stupid she plays her cards right from the start, so it is not really surprising that she is applauded for her organizing abilities and devotion to the cause.

This Queen is sure to be found in every office and place of work. Age does not matter, for both young and old alike play the same overbearing role, with a result that they are known as witches and worse. Regarded as a difficult, bossy and thoroughly dangerous woman she sees herself as a dutiful, honest and forthright person who is greatly wronged by everyone, including her family.

Psychological Significance

Hard-hearted and headstrong this character lacks every trace of feminine warmth. Inhibited emotions cause frustration which adds to the outer veneer of ruthlessness. A close relationship with the opposite sex is desperately needed, but there are few men who feel inclined to take her on. When they do the partnership does not last long.

Psychic Significance
In the past this Queen would have been recognized as a witch whose practices were suspect to say the least. Considerable occult knowledge gives her power over those who become her initiates and, once in her clutches, it is virtually impossible to escape.

Influential Significance
This is a ruthless influence lacking all compassion and wisdom. It is reminiscent of the iron hand in the velvet glove which delivers blows swiftly and passes on silently leaving behind confusion and disruption. Good may result from this havoc eventually, but this will depend on other factors as well. Beware of the person who helps others into trouble.

Reversed Significance
Selfishness develops into a rigid characteristic that blots out every trace of feeling for others. As a female recluse, everyone keeps well away for fear of being attacked verbally, if not physically. Loneliness is inevitable, but this woman is her own worst enemy.

JACK OF SPADES

The Jack's Significance
This card rarely represents a boy but if it does it depicts a delinquent. As a man it symbolizes an emotionally immature, inadequate and totally impracticable person. He is misinformed and is misinforming so his word and advice should never be relied upon. Even so, he is full of self-importance, self-confidence and big ideas. As he grows older he lives more and more in a world of his own.

Practical Significance
Although this man lacks authority, he takes it upon himself to boss others. This does not make for popularity but he has only himself to blame. Insincerity in the past has given him a bad reputation, so when it comes to promotion at work he is passed over. Friends are few and far between but, since 'birds of a feather flock together', those he has are unreliable and devious. They are the proverbial dogs who have been given a bad name so it is difficult to shake off this bad image. This Jack is usually the leader of the gang.

As a husband he is hard going for any woman who is foolish enough to have him. A Queen of spades is the only one who has any degree of control over him, but this is never a happy arrangement. Should a romantic Queen of hearts misguidedly take him on, she will rue the day and every succeeding day she stays with him. His mother and older women are the only ones who have any time for him. Maybe this is because his mentality remains that of a spoilt child all his life.

Psychological Significance
Gross emotional immaturity is the cause of this mixed-up character. Inner turmoil manifests outwardly as aggression and wanton behaviour. Leadership qualities are only temporary and disappear altogether with increasing years.

Psychic Significance
Entering the psychic scene like a flash of lightning, all attention focusses on this startling newcomer. But thunder will surely follow and these rumblings should arouse suspicions, so beware of him. He will certainly have a few tricks up his sleeve, but only the naive and gullible will be taken in.

Influential Significance
This disturbing influence brings out the worst in individuals and magnifies the negative aspects in every situation. Everything will be revealed through this, so expect secrets to be thrown to the wind and confidences to be broken. Courage is needed to face up to all this, but to compensate there is a feeling of distinct relief.

Reversed Significance
A thoroughly despicable character like this should not expect

much from anyone. Untrustworthy and unreliable he is shunned and lonely. At work he is avoided and in the home he receives little love since he gives little in return. When confronted with his own mistakes and faults he flies into a childish rage.

TEN OF SPADES

Numerical Significance
The tenth card in this suit completes a round in life which has been difficult to say the least. From this point things can only get better. Looking back on events shows how things went in circles with nothing accomplished in the end. Even a downward spiral may be discovered, from which it will take time to recover, but as an obstacle course this phase has ended.

Practical Significance
Personal frustration is to be expected as a result of past and present circumstances, so tears and jealousy are excusable although they do nothing to solve things. Enthusiasm and hopes are likely to be dashed to the ground so do not expect too much yet. Difficulties with practical plans, emotional hopes and money matters bring delays and minor upsets. Communication proves to be a major problem which causes misunderstandings all round.

Loss of jobs and failure to find new ones take their toll on emotions and domestic scenes suffer from intolerance and frayed nerves as a result. Relationships naturally become tense so watch out for trouble spots which trigger off fiery reactions. This is generally a negative card; therefore every possible precaution should be taken, on every level, to keep things on an even keel. This will be a lone task and it will be difficult to recognize true friends but, if it is of any comfort, many are in the same boat with you. An end to the present trouble is in sight, so keep going.

Psychological Significance
Depth of depression are reached through external circum-

stances. This is understandable but it must not develop into a regular response pattern where every obstacle, however small, triggers off this extremely negative reaction.

Psychic Significance

Occult work in a group faces a severe challenge. The weakest link in the chain places everyone in danger, so whoever this person is must be discovered, psychically cleared and re-aligned. Strengthen protection against external, interfering forces which seek to break up a circle trying to work harmoniously.

Influential Significance

Enthusiasm will be drastically dampened down by this negative influence. Any lack of drive must be fought and overcome if survival on practical, emotional and financial fronts is to be maintained. Stick to original plans until something better turns up, which it will shortly. Beware of misunderstandings which could trigger off a long chain of events which blight the future.

Reversed Significance

Just when things look to be at their worst they deteriorate even more. A rough ride, going over the same old ground frustrates to breaking point. It is difficult to see where all this will lead as the wheel of fate continues to turn much as it did before.

NINE OF SPADES

Numerical Significance

The ninth card in this suit is consistant in that it keeps up its promise of further negativity. An all-time low is reached which affects any one of the three other suits representing practical, emotional and financial matters. Even so, everything happening now helps to clear the air but this will be realized only after the event and when the edge has worn off a painful memory. Numerically, it is still a fortunate number if only because it prevents an even worse fate.

Practical Significance

Worries over health and, to a lesser extent, wealth drain energy, allowing depression to take over. A stage is reached where action must be taken so whatever happens, expect something of a change. Illnesses will be brought to light and revealed for what they are; these range from minor complaints to conditions needing urgent medical attention. Suspense comes to an end and with this comparative peace of mind, as long-feared enemies are recognized for what they are.

Scandals and idle gossip bring unhappiness to many innocent people. Although this could result a long time after the event which started off the negative trail, it still causes suffering. It is important to try to rise above these difficult circumstances, as impossible as it seems and above all, conserve personal energy. This is the key to solving all trouble, physical and mental, so rest and relax whenever possible. Beware of wasting valuable energy on trivialities that do not really matter and ignore pettiness in others for this is a trap which distracts from the main issue.

Psychological Significance

Lack of energy lowers resistance to everything. Apart from feeling under the weather physically, the emotional threshold to stress is so weakened that a break-down is on the cards. It is far better to do nothing rather than do the wrong thing, because this simply piles on the agony.

Psychic Significance

Occult battles with negative forces test defences. Rituals involving astral projection should not be attempted at this stage for fear of a serious attack. Watch out for danger signals inside as well as outside the group or circle, which seek to cause a rift.

Influential Significance

As a negative influence of a parasitic nature this will deplete even the strongest characters. Beware of wasting energy on self-pity and self-recrimination as a result of this; instead, reverse the process into positive thinking and planning. Tiredness and lack of drive unite into a destructive partnership and, if allowed to continue, they demolish every hope for the future.

Reversed Significance

Serious troubles associated with poor health and lack of wealth bring increasing bouts of depression. Help is no longer offered because it has been rejected in the past. Underhand schemes to make money fail and, even worse, past devious plans designed to extract profits by undesirable means will be exposed. Further misery results.

EIGHT OF SPADES

Numerical Significance

The eighth card in this suit is negative and most unfortunate, causing disputes which are extremely difficult to understand, let alone resolve. This is because only half the picture can be seen at any one time and somewhere between the two lies a no man's land where there is nothing to win and nothing to lose either. This is a thoroughly frustrating situation which cannot be ignored.

Practical Significance

Obstacles and indecisions rule over every aspect of life. Business schemes, travel arrangements, including holidays and ambitions for the future suffer particularly so expect delays before matters are sorted out satisfactorily. In arguments, both points of view are evenly matched, making it virtually impossible to make progress but, sooner or later, the scales will tip one way and end the present deadlock. Time must not be wasted during this temporary lull, so use this to prepare for the final fray and the action which is bound to follow. No good will come from forcing the issue at this stage so sit tight.

On the domestic front there will be clashes within the family probably between younger and older members. Love-affairs will face a testing time too and only the really well adjusted relationships will survive. A strong warning is also given with this card concerning trust. Do not reveal personal secrets nor give away confidential information relating to other people to anyone.

There is a possibility of enforced isolation such as a stay in hospital or, in extreme cases, it could be a prison sentence. Whichever it is, this should be taken as an opportunity to recover from personal difficulties. It will also act as a future safeguard and protection.

Psychological Significance

Definite strength of will exists, but without a specific aim this is like a journey without a destination. Make sure that an end object is in view and that mental energy is properly controlled and directed towards this. Intellectual powers will be wasted too, unless a strict discipline and routine is laid down and kept to.

Psychic Significance

Beware of working in the dark both literally and metaphorically. Lone workers are in particular danger of an occult attack since they lack protection from a psychic partner or from a group. These attacks will take unexpected and unusual forms and will by no means be confined to psychic levels only.

Influential Significance

This influence frustrates the individual by placing obstacles in the way and brings wheels within wheels grinding to a halt. Attempts to communicate with others fail, so take advantage of this uneasy quiet to make watertight plans and better policies in readiness. Strained emotional relationships run the risk of reaching breaking point, especially if enemies have a chance to have their say.

Reversed Significance

No good will come from a scheme, in spite of all the effort and hard work put into it. This leads to despondency, depression and dejection which does not lift easily. Lack of self-confidence does little to help an already bad situation.

SEVEN OF SPADES

Numerical Significance

The seventh card in this suit has strong personal associations of a distinctly negative nature. Secret fears and worries cast despondent shadows over the brightest scenes and bad characteristics are allowed to express themselves. These override compassion from the heart and logic from the head. Individual selfishness rules and will continue to do so until a realistic and honest approach to life is adopted.

Practical Significance

Although personal worries exist, they are no excuse for bad manners and hasty tempers. By allowing fears of what might happen to control and colour every aspect of life, a dark cloud hangs over the present. Eventually this will bring a depletion of energy, and invite more trouble in the form of physical illness and depression.

There is a risk that attitudes to life become increasingly selfish and, although rarely recognized as this, other people see it all too clearly. Negative situations are attracted to negative people, so much of the present trouble could have been avoided. Practical and emotional problems may well exist but these can become complicated through wrong thinking and consequent wrong handling. Disputes with friends and workmates are unavoidable and these strike deep at the roots of individual standpoint. Obstacles and misfortunes, however, are necessary experiences meant to teach lessons in living, but the present chain of negative events is being fostered by a poor philosophy and understanding of what life is all about.

Psychological Significance

Difficulty in altering fixed patterns of thought form a barrier around the mind which blinkers the sight. Expansion and expression of the personality is inhibited and an altogether bigoted character develops. If freed from this self-imposed bond, a new positive life-style develops and one way to begin to do this is to seek out a good basic philosophy.

Psychic Significance
Insufficient belief in powers beyond this world must be reconciled with the continued pursuit of psychic phenomena. It is extremely dangerous to venture further along the occult path without complete acceptance of these, plus recognition of symbols and archetypes. Rebound reactions are to be expected until a definite conclusion is reached.

Influential Significance
Personal problems reach a crisis point as a result of this influence. Worries concerning health, the family or matters at work cast gloom over everything else. Fears will be exaggerated and although most of these will never happen, they still have the power to produce a negative atmosphere and interfere with peace of mind. Control has never been more necessary than now, because things could deteriorate even more if left to their own devices.

Reversed Significance
Spite and malice are fostered like vipers in the bosom. Seeing life as an errand of vengeance can only reap more disasterous reactions, so until it is realized that one negative action produces another negative reaction, things will continue on the downward path until rock-bottom is reached.

SIX OF SPADES

Numerical Significance
The sixth card in this suit represents hard work which shows little reward for all the effort. Attempts to preserve that which has already been achieved will meet with opposition, but the fight must continue. There are always two aspects to be considered and these have to be manoeuvred into a position which produces some degree of equilibrium.

Practical Significance

Disappointments are inevitable, but this does not mean all is lost. Although a 'wet blanket' atmosphere dampens down enthusiasm, in no way does it extinguish the spark of ingenuity so there is still hope. Set-backs such as this, when viewed in retrospect, will be seen to have been for the best.

Minor health problems will prevent complete fulfilment of plans, but again, all will be for the best so do not waste time and energy worrying about what might have been. Depression is likely but this should not be allowed to overshadow the hatching of plans for the future. From a practical point of view, just when contracts concerning property are about to be signed, along come doubts and everything stops short. Diplomacy and time will work wonders in this situation whereas attempts to force the issue will only make things worse. Have faith and wait for a change in circumstances which will be for the better.

Psychological Significance

Difficulties in reconciling the inner realm of dreams with the outer world of harsh realities causes mental conflict. One without the other is incomplete and therefore unfulfilling, so the answer lies in a blend of the two. These two aspects represent the conscious and unconscious minds, between which there should exist strong links.

Psychic Significance

Forces beyond control impose self-sacrifice that greatly disturb psychic workers. Those who operate alone are in particular danger. Difficulties with astral projection will be the first warning sign, followed by garbled messages from outerspace.

Influential Significance

This influence brings disappointment, tears and set-backs. Even when things seem to be going really well, a negative feeling manages to creep in and spoil everything. Undercover actions are suspected although there is no proof that they exist. Matters will improve shortly but meanwhile, be prepared for delays, unexpected obstacles and being let down by others.

Reversed Significance
News which should have arrived some time ago arrives too late to prevent a catastrophe. Obstacles now seem like permanent fixtures and trying to escape from them is impossible, certainly at the moment. A long chain of disasters, fortunately none of which are devastating, look like continuing for some time.

FIVE OF SPADES

Numerical Significance
The fifth card in this suit has the power to demolish every hope that once stood a good chance of succeeding. Misunderstandings and misinterpretations have laid a false trail leading to the downward path. Aims and ambitions for the future must not be lost, in spite of the present obstacles because this is a testing–time. Those who emerge will greatly increase their strength and understanding of life. Personal involvement with certain unpleasant situations cannot be avoided and it will mean carrying other people's burdens.

Practical Significance
This card warns against discouragement. Although trouble seems to heap upon trouble, there is still a bright spot on the horizon. Success is still within the grasp, so long as it is sought with courage and determination. Whatever the odds, try hard to see it through to the end and do not give up now.

Plans for a career, business projects, holidays and moving house are all at risk due to temporary set-backs, but last minute reprieves suddenly put everything right again.

Money matters take a knocking but again final calculations will show them to be far better than was feared. On the emotional level, relationships will suffer from misunderstandings which complicate things so much that there is a risk of a complete break. By accepting the inevitable and flowing with the stream there will be an improvement of circumstances, but do not expect to solve difficulties easily for this is impossible. Original plans and hopes should not be allowed to become submerged beneath the present trouble. Confidence and strength is needed to carry on, so concentrate on the future and not on past regrets. Accept that everything is going to take that much longer than was first thought and reorganize the calendar to fit in with the new schedule. Once this is done there will be a feeling of relief at having tried to do something about the situation.

Psychological Significance
Beware of speaking your mind in the so-called name of honesty. Brutal truths should be delivered with discretion and more often than not they should be replaced with white lies anyway. It is not a sign of a strong character to be able to tell others their fortunes in this way.

Psychic Significance
Entities from the lower astral plane masquerade as innocent spirits. These test the power of challenge and call for accurate recognition of signs, symbols, archetypes and all unseen forces. Use the pentacle, the five-pointed star, for protection.

Influential Significance
This influence has the power to complicate and disrupt even the simplest of plans. On the positive side it will single out unseen obstacles which are better brought to light now than later so in this sense it is not bad. Eventual success is on the cards, but only after difficulties have been ironed out. Doubt and lack of faith in ones own ability is also introduced with this influence so see it as a real personal challenge.

Reversed Significance
Beware of the stab in the back which could have far-reaching disasterous effects. This may result from the past, so try to put an end to a negative chain of events before it reaps more havoc. Legal battles will prove costly and in the end nothing will have been proved. Try to avoid such action.

FOUR OF SPADES

Numerical Significance

The fourth card in this suit combines an unstable number with the negativity of the suit as a whole. The effect from this is to halt previous progress in different ways and create trouble all round. Battles are foreseen and these range from court cases down to battles of wits.

Practical Significance

Legal battles, arguments and disputes are to be expected. Watertight cases suddenly spring a leak and everything looks like collapsing. The weakest link in the chain should be found and examined carefully for signs of trouble and, small though these may be, they have the power to wreck everything. Practical, emotional and financial plans will all be affected. Love-affairs will develop into frustrating experiences especially if clandestine meetings are involved. As a warning, divorce or separation is on the cards. Unfortunately, there is little one can do about the present situation except wait and see.

A rest from worry and strife should be considered, which is not the same as trying to escape personal responsibilities. Health problems could be an added burden so this must be preserved above all else. Loss of sleep from worry could start a viscious circle, ending in either physical or mental illness, so make sure a good night's rest is a regular occurrence. Relax during the day-time whenever possible.

Psychological Significance

Primitive instincts should be recognized as such and therefore controlled. These go with mundane pursuits and whilst they continue to rule, intellect and wisdom, let alone compassion, do not have a look-in. Brute force and ignorance lead to self-imposed imprisonment.

Psychic Significance

Be prepared for a battle with occult forces. Difficulties in knowing the enemy, who will be heavily disguised, confuse and disrupt the harmony within the group. Long-term after-effects will further disturb and bring trouble but at least it will sort the sheep from the goats.

Influential Significance

This influence introduces a heartless atmosphere. Disputes arising from business and matrimonial affairs could end in court and in lengthy legal battles. On a less formidable level, troubles will be brought into the open where they can be dealt with fairly and squarely. Although unpleasant at the time, the air will be cleared as a result.

Reversed Significance

Lack of courage does nothing to help the present wave of trouble. Ignoring the true facts only postpones the final outcome and this gets worse the longer it is left. Delaying tactics should not be tried and although this may seem one way out it is, in fact, only putting off the evil moment.

THREE OF SPADES

Numerical Significance

The third card in this suit represents a three-sided problem which undermines stability and equality. Emotional relationships and business partnerships are particularly susceptible as a third person or principle tries to interfere with the present harmony. Destructive forces seek to destroy long-established arrangements and will often try to do this in the name of progress.

Practical Significance

This card symbolizes the eternal triangle, a situation that can never be a happy arrangement. When relating to marriage and business partnerships no stability or progress will ever be made whilst this unsatisfactory structure exists. A blind eye may be turned to an ever increasing threat but this cannot be swept under the carpet forever. Eventually, the truth will out.

As a warning, every precaution should be taken when considering a third partner for he or she may sooner or later throw a spanner in the works. On emotional levels a third person enters the scene who has the power to disrupt an old-established relationship. This is usually presumed to be a secret lover but the culprit might be a child or relative who proves the theory that two are company but three is a crowd. Even an obsession which one of the partners has for a hobby or sport could be the third interloper but whoever or whatever it is, it will take three times as much effort to keep the status quo.

Psychological Significance
Creative thoughts are self-inhibited so the result is third-rate work and lack of originality. A complete change in attitude, not only to work but to life as a whole is needed, but this must be voluntary and not something imposed by a third party.

Psychic Significance
Beware of matriarchal tyranny ruling through emotional blackmail, mental enslavement and jealousy. This will be cleverly done so do not expect the obvious. Feminine vibrations of a destructive nature must be anticipated and, as destructive as these are, they will not be easily recognized.

Influential Significance
This influence introduces a third aspect which thoroughly upsets plans and relationships. Arguments develop and there is the likelihood of great enmity stemming from a once harmonious situation. The breaking of agreements is likely and applies to emotional commitments as well as to business pledges. As an early warning sign look for an atmosphere of aggression.

Reversed Significance
The breaking of an agreement can lead to personal strife and collectively to group or even national hostility. Action of a most despicable nature is taken and this is not done in the name of humanity. Disorder rules in place of harmony, so the future looks bleak and without a lot of hope for some time to come.

TWO OF SPADES

Numerical Significance

The second card in this suit brings duality and opposition. Complications arise and the disharmony produced by this has the power to sever long-standing relationships and agreements. Indecision delays everything with stalemate situations on emotional, practical and financial fronts. Neither side of the fence offers a balanced solution so wait for further developments before taking the next step.

Practical Significance

This card warns of a dividing of the ways but there is little to choose from either path. Split into two, neither half is complete within itself so difficulties will undoubtedly develop. These will grow unless the situation is faced, understood and accepted. Then, and only then should further moves be considered. A change in direction will bring the present stalemate to an end but determination and patience are needed to do this. Expect the depths of depression on the one hand, but hope on the other because from this point the only way out is up.

Emotional relationships will be charged with disharmony through clashes of temperament and business partnerships will suffer from opposing views. Separate ways are on the cards but there is no reason why these paths should not unite in the future when both parties are on the same track again.

Since this card represents an all-time low everything associated with it can only be described as negative too. Seen symbolically as the last week of winter, spring cannot be far behind.

Psychological Significance

Obsessions reach a peak or trough, as the case may be. The truth is distorted out of all proportion as complete fantasy takes over. There is a danger of entering a dream world from which there is no escape and no return.

Psychic Significance
The dangers of evoking names of power are realized too late.
Dual forces clash causing psychic fireworks and a chain reaction is started which encircles and enslaves those who first
sought to raise them.

Influential Significance
This influence negates and opposes all hopes and plans for the
future. Indecisions and uncertainty shatter personal confidence, so balanced outlooks suddenly suffer a split down the
middle causing confusion and depression. In all relationships,
both sides will find that this influence highlights their partners
defects which leads to more trouble. Since plans become
impossible to fulfil and finances are greatly reduced, hibernate
mentally and wait for the first breath of spring.

Reversed Significance
This card represents the depths of depression and despair.
Deliberate and downright bad intentions have produced
negativity, so gloom and darkness overshadows everything.
As the dark night of the soul, all hope seems to have gone but a
final chance to redress the balance will be offered soon.

21

THE JOKER

The Joker's Significance

This card is not numbered but traditionally it is represented as zero, a sign embracing all and nothing, sense and nonsense, happiness and sadness and wisdom and folly. Looking at this lively figure it is difficult to decide exactly what his message is until, that is, it is realized that he is in disguise. His costume is that of a court jester, a buffoon who was supposed to make a King laugh. A jester, however, was far from a fool and in this lies the Joker's secret.

Practical Significance

This card symbolizes individual potential latent within each of us which may or may not express itself fully during one lifetime. On the surface, this appears as the innocence of a child, the wisdom of Job, the stupidity of an idiot or as pure tomfoolcry but whichever it is, it has the power to deceive and take others by surprise.

Progress in practical and financial affairs can confidently be expected as unlimited energy drives on towards a most satisfactory conclusion. Powers to transform are at work so anything is possible as new life is given to flagging projects. Emotionally, an unexpected experience has a profound effect on relationships and, whether happy or disillusioning, it certainly throws a new light onto the whole affair. Intellectually, a flash of brilliance and originality brings success to those striving for academic awards and again, this comes out of the blue.

Untapped energy and individual possibilities express themselves when least expected with a result that lives and situations could be transformed overnight. A carefree attitude replaces an old cautious approach, making life much easier to face, if nothing else.

Psychological Significance

Here is the eccentric who harbours the seeds of a genius but these will grow only if sown in a conventional way. In doing this lies the difficulty. Unable to accept society as it is, he or she attempts to alter it but, since this cannot be done without first becoming part of that establishment, the task seems impossible. The Joker, however, is a clever juggler too and takes everyone, including himself, by surprise!

Psychic Significance

A psychic awakening opens the door on a new dimension and the journey into another world has begun. Seeking enlightenment in this way reveals the path of the mystic and this is one strewn with pitfalls and rewards but, above all, surprises.

Influential Significance

Expect the unexpected with this influence. Surprises will alter situations in a flash, bringing last minute help, changes in fortune, recovery from illnesses and instant friendship, both platonic as well as romantic. Be prepared for sudden illogical events involving people and circumstances that are most unusual and perhaps comical.

Reversed Significance

Living up to the ordinary reputation of the Joker, expect status to be downgraded to the level of a fool, a vagabond and a mindless seeker of pleasure. There is indeed nothing much of a character beneath a superficial top dressing.

INDEX